Shakespeare

and the Stuff of Life

Shakespeare

and the Stuff of Life

Treasures from the
Shakespeare Birthplace Trust

Edited by

DELIA GARRATT AND
TARA HAMLING

Bloomsbury Arden Shakespeare
An imprint of Bloomsbury Publishing Plc

BLOOMSBURY
LONDON · OXFORD · NEW YORK · NEW DELHI · SYDNEY

Bloomsbury Arden Shakespeare

An imprint of Bloomsbury Publishing Plc

Imprint previously known as Arden Shakespeare

50 Bedford Square	1385 Broadway
London	New York
WC1B 3DP	NY 10018
UK	USA

www.bloomsbury.com

BLOOMSBURY, THE ARDEN SHAKESPEARE and the Diana logo are trademarks of Bloomsbury Publishing Plc

First published 2016

© The Shakespeare Birthplace Trust

British Library Cataloguing-in-Publication Data

A catalogue record for this book is available from the British Library.

ISBN: PB: 978-1-4742-2226-6

Library of Congress Cataloging-in-Publication Data

A catalog record for this book is available from the Library of Congress.

Typeset by RefineCatch Limited, Bungay, Suffolk
Printed and bound in India

Published in association with the Shakespeare Birthplace Trust

Contents

Foreword x
Acknowledgements xi
List of contributors xii
Introduction xiii

I

Birth

1   St George and the Dragon 2
2   Carved wooden angel 5
3   Chrismatory 6
4   *Book of Common Prayer* and Psalter 9
5   Corporation mace 10
6   Pike head 13
7   Cloak clasp 14
8   'Cubborde of Boxes' 17
9   Map of Warwickshire and Leicestershire 18
10   Pocket atlas 21

2

Childhood

11 Painting of a Mother and
Child 25

12 Highchair 26

13 Wooden doll 29

14 Hornbook 30

15 Ovid's *Metamorphoses* 33

16 *The History of Four-Footed
Beasts* 34

17 Tortoise-shell box 37

3

Youth

18 Gloves 40

19 Sword 43

20 Bodice 44

21 Thimble 47

22 Sweet bag 48

4

Marriage and Domestic Life

23 Painted cloth 52

24 Carved knife sheath 55

25 Wooden chest 56

26 The 'Hathaway Bed' 59

27 Long cushion cover 60

28 An allegorical painting 63

29 Painting of a kitchen scene 64

30 Painting of 'A Family Saying Grace Before A Meal' 67

31 Cauldron 68

32 Joint-stool 71

33 'Bartmann' jug 72

5

Professional Life

34 View of London Bridge 76

35 *Venus and Adonis* 79

36 Money box 80

37 Painting of 'Wee Three Loggerheads' 83

38 Writing desk box 84

39 A letter to Shakespeare 87

6

Older Age

40 William Shakespeare's seal-ring? 90

41 A die from New Place 93

42 Gentleman's nightcap 94

43 Posset cup 97

44 Banqueting trencher 98

45 Pocket dial 101

7

Death

46 Memento mori seal impression 104

47 Painting of 'Death and the Maiden' 107

48 Medicine chest 108

49 Parish register 111

50 Shakespeare's bust 112

Key dates in the life of William Shakespeare 114

Credits and references 115

Foreword

THE SHAKESPEARE BIRTHPLACE TRUST cares for Shakespeare's five family homes in Stratford-upon-Avon and for one of the world's most important Shakespeare collections seeking to make them accessible for people from around the globe through award-winning educational programmes, through research, exhibitions and online. Spanning over 800 years of history, the breadth of the collection is extraordinary and it reveals much about Shakespeare the man, his life, the times in which he lived and the works he wrote. Without doubt, it is the combination of material culture, performance and local historical context that makes these collections unique and so important. In particular, the Trust holds an outstanding collection of works of art, crafted items and printed works dating from the early modern period, which provides an insight into the world that Shakespeare and his contemporaries would have experienced.

This book develops from a long-standing knowledge exchange partnership with the University of Birmingham which has produced a wealth of new information and interpretation around these sixteenth- and seventeenth-century objects, many that are now rare and little-known, but which would once have been a familiar part of the visual and material culture of Shakespeare's world. The book uses this new research – bringing many of the vivid and intriguing stories behind these objects to life.

Dr Diana Owen, Chief Executive of the
Shakespeare Birthplace Trust

Acknowledgements

THE RESEARCH THAT INFORMS THIS book develops from a collaboration between collections staff at the Shakespeare Birthplace Trust and researchers in History and the Shakespeare Institute at the University of Birmingham. This work has been made possible thanks to the formal support provided by an Arts and Humanities Research Council Collaborative Doctorate held by Peter Hewitt (2010–13) and informally through the generosity and dedication of all involved to share information and improve understanding of the sixteenth- and seventeenth-century treasures held in the SBT collections, most notably through an online blog series 'Shakespeare's World in 100 Objects'. We would like to thank the contributors to the volume for embracing this collaborative project with such enthusiasm. Many colleagues have supported or inspired research that underpins the approach and contents of this book; we would like to acknowledge a debt, in particular, to Ann Donnelly, Richard Cust, Michael Dobson, Paul Edmondson, David Hopes, Kate McLuskie, Jennifer Reid, Catherine Richardson, Kate Rumbold, Rosalyn Sklar, Andrew Thomas and Martin Wiggins as well as members of the Centre for Reformation and Early Modern Studies at the University of Birmingham. Finally, we are grateful to Margaret Bartley at Bloomsbury for her enthusiasm and guidance in producing this publication.

List of contributors

Stephanie Appleton is a Doctoral Researcher at the University of Birmingham. Her thesis examines the community of Stratford-upon-Avon in the sixteenth and seventeenth centuries, with a particular focus on the town's women.

Delia Garratt is Director of Cultural Engagement at the Shakespeare Birthplace Trust. She received her doctorate from the University of Leicester in 2002. Her work in museums has focused on making collections more widely accessible.

Tara Hamling is Senior Lecturer in History and Associate Fellow of the Shakespeare Institute at the University of Birmingham. She has published widely on the visual and material culture of Tudor and Stuart England.

Peter Hewitt completed his PhD in the material culture of early modern England with the University of Birmingham in 2014. He is now Manager of the Museum of Witchcraft and Magic in Boscastle, Cornwall.

Victoria Jackson is Lecturer in History at the Open University. She completed her University of Birmingham doctoral thesis on the material culture of dining in early modern England in 2014.

Elizabeth Sharrett is a 2014 Shakespeare Institute graduate where she completed her doctoral thesis on the use of beds as stage properties in Renaissance drama, which she is adapting for publication as a monograph.

Introduction

H ISTORIC CRAFTED OBJECTS PROVIDE AN immediate, evoc-
ative insight into the needs, beliefs and behaviours of people in the
past. The rich legacy of surviving artefacts from the time of Shakespeare
makes tangible the major themes of this period of history, such as: religious and social change, discovery and exploration, education, rites of
passage (birth, marriage, death), family and domestic life, professional and
community life, status and lifestyle.

We have selected 50 objects from the collections of the Shakespeare
Birthplace Trust and grouped them in seven sections to reflect popular
ideas surrounding the lifecycle in Elizabethan and Jacobean England.
Shakespeare and his contemporaries were familiar with a long tradition of
the 'Ages of Man' where the passage of life was divided into various phases.
These Ages are outlined in a monologue spoken by the melancholy Jaques
in *As You Like It*, Act 2 Scene 7. The speech compares the world to a stage
and life to the acts of a play:

> All the world's a stage,
> And all the men and women merely players.
> They have their exits and their entrances,
> And one man in his time plays many parts,
> His acts being seven ages.
>
> (2.7.139–42)

1. BIRTH:

> At first the infant,
> Mewling and puking in the nurse's arms.
>
> (2.7.143–4)

The first 10 objects represent the birth of a new world and the processes of religious, social and intellectual change that were underway in 1564 when Shakespeare was born. We start with objects reflecting the religious reforms of the period then consider items reflecting civic life in Shakespeare's home town of Stratford-upon-Avon; like many of his contemporaries, Shakespeare's father was directly involved with changes to systems of faith and governance. Also in this group are objects reflecting the ways in which the wider world was opening up for ordinary Elizabethans, with a new sense of local, national and global geographies communicated through print.

2. CHILDHOOD:

> Then, the whining school-boy with his satchel
> And shining morning face, creeping like snail
> Unwillingly to school.
>
> (2.7.145–7)

These objects reflect the stuff of childhood – toys, educational tools and curious texts and treasures to stimulate the imaginations of Shakespeare's generation.

3. YOUTH:

> And then the lover,
> sighing like furnace, with a woeful ballad
> Made to his mistress' eyebrow.
>
> (2.7.147–9)

Here we consider clothing and gifts that catered to youthful swagger, showing off, love and courtship.

4. MARRIAGE AND FAMILY:

>   the justice,
> In fair round belly, a good capon lin'd,
> With eyes severe, and beard of formal cut,
> Full of wise saws, and modern instances,
> And so he plays his part.
>
> (2.7.153–7)

Jaques' speech has the justice as the fifth age but Shakespeare married and had children early in his life so he had to take on this role of respectable patriarch unusually young. We have therefore switched the fourth and fifth age around for the purposes of this volume. The objects in this Age reflect the significance of marriage as the founding of a household, and the vulnerability of this institution due to suspicions around female sexuality. Also in this section are some of the ordinary, humble, domestic objects that came to be associated with popular beliefs around witchcraft and the supernatural.

5. PROFESSIONAL LIFE:

>   Then, a soldier,
> Full of strange oaths, and bearded like the pard,
> Jealous in honour, sudden and quick in quarrel,
> Seeking the bubble reputation
> Even in the cannon's mouth.
>
> (2.7.149–53)

As far as we know, Shakespeare was never a soldier but he sought and gained honour and reputation as poet, actor, playwright and businessman.

These objects relate to Shakespeare's career as writer and partner in the playhouse industry in London where the printing trade and new purpose-built theatres supported his talents and ambitions.

6.   OLDER AGE:

The sixth age shifts
Into the lean and slippered pantaloon,
With spectacles on nose and pouch on side

(2.7.157–9)

In the later years of his life, Shakespeare was well established as a gentleman of Stratford-upon-Avon, where he lived in a grand town house called New Place. The objects included here are associated with privileged gentry status and evoke the kind of lifestyle Shakespeare might have enjoyed at home in his 'sixth age'.

7.   DEATH:

Last scene of all,
That ends this strange eventful history,
Is second childishness and mere oblivion,
Sans teeth, *sans* eyes, *sans* taste, *sans* everything.

(2.7.163–6)

In Shakespearean England there was a rich tradition of using images and objects to encourage people to meditate on and prepare for death. This last group of objects reflects this trend. The final few objects are a tangible record of Shakespeare's own death, on 23 April 1616 at the age of 52.

Figure 0.1 Page from the so-called 'First Folio': 'Mr. William Shakespeares comedies, histories, & tragedies. Published according to the true originall copies', 1623, London, approx 22cm × 36cm, SBT 8300002X (SR 37).

Ia. All the world's a stage,
And all the men and women, meerely Players;
They haue their *Exits* and their Entrances,
And one man in his time playes many parts,
His Acts being seuen ages. At first the Infant,
Mewling, and puking in the Nurses armes:
Then, the whining Schoole-boy with his Satchell
And shining morning face, creeping like snaile
Vnwillingly to schoole. And then the Louer,
Sighing like Furnace, with a wofull ballad
Made to his Mistresse eye-brow. Then, a Soldier,
Full of strange oaths, and bearded like the Pard,
Ielous in honor, sodaine, and quicke in quarrell,
Seeking the bubble Reputation
Euen in the Canons mouth: And then, the Iustice,
In faire round belly, with good Capon lin'd,
With eyes seuere, and beard of formall cut,
Full of wise sawes, and moderne instances,
And so he playes his part. The sixt age shifts
Into the leane and slipper'd Pantaloone,
With spectacles on nose, and pouch on side,
His youthfull hose well sau'd, a world too wide,
For his shrunke shanke, and his bigge manly voice,
Turning againe toward childish trebble pipes,
And whistles in his sound. Last Scene of all,
That ends this strange euentfull historie,
Is second childishnesse, and meere obliuion,
Sans teeth, sans eyes, sans taste, sans euery thing.

Birth I

St George and the Dragon   no. 1

THIS IS A COLOURED PRINT of one of the medieval wall paintings that once decorated the Guild Chapel in Shakespeare's home town of Stratford-upon-Avon. It depicts St George, the heroic warrior saint and, from 1350, patron saint of England. He is shown according to legend as defeating a terrifying dragon, symbol of evil. The print was made around 1804 following the discovery of the fifteenth-century paintings under layers of whitewash.

The image represents the changing world into which William Shakespeare was born. The Elizabethan religious settlement of 1559 had finally, after decades of turmoil, established Protestantism as the official state religion. This faith required major changes to church space to remove traditional sacred materials associated with late-medieval Catholicism. Images of saints were banned in churches because reformers believed they distracted people from true worship, which should be directed to God. The vivid images of holy characters and miracles that had adorned churches for centuries were now gradually removed and there was a new emphasis on reading and hearing the Bible in English.

John Shakespeare, as town chamberlain, supervised the 'defacing' of images in Stratford's Guild Chapel in 1563, the year before his son was born. William was baptised on 26 April 1564 and, as it was usual to baptise infants a few days after birth, it is commonly accepted he was born on the 23 April. The date happens to be St George's day, which had traditionally been celebrated with fairs, processions and plays. While the celebration of his feast day was gradually phased out in most areas during Shakespeare's lifetime, the Saint continued to provide a focus for patriotic pride.

Figure 1.1 Print showing a medieval fresco in the Guild Chapel, Stratford-upon-Avon, depicting battle between St George and the Dragon, by Thomas Fisher, print from drawing, c.1804, 52cm × 45cm, SBT 1994-19/15.

Carved wooden angel

THIS MASTERPIECE OF ENGLISH MEDIEVAL carving once stood high in the roof-space of the Guild Chapel in Stratford-upon-Avon. Dating to the 1450s, it is an example of a 'feathered' angel, and is extremely rare in Western art. Whilst most angels are represented with wings but essentially human, wearing clothes, this angel is covered with feathers. It wears a cap decorated with a pointed cross, and its expression is both distant and serene. The hands are raised in a gesture of protection or acceptance.

Guilds were social and religious organizations for traders or craftsmen within a town. Their chapels provided divine services for the souls of guild members and their ancestors. This angel was part of the grand interior decoration of Stratford's Guild Chapel which was beautified around 1449 with new furnishings. It would have been brightly painted and was probably placed upon a central beam on the chancel arch above the high altar.

Wooden statues of angels often adorned the roofspace of churches, chapels and the great halls of manor houses in the later medieval period. They represented the protective quality of heavenly angels in watching over human affairs and fending off evil spirits. While images of saints and holy figures were forbidden in Protestant places of worship, these lofty statues of angels were not removed in the first phases of the Reformation (in part because they were hard to reach) and would still have been visible in Shakespeare's lifetime. His plays refer to their protective role, as when Hamlet sees the ghost of his father and exclaims, 'Angels and ministers of grace defend us!' (1.4.39).

Figure 1.2 Carved figure of an angel, English, 15th century, oak, 90 cm, SBT 1865-2/1.

Chrismatory *no. 3*

S MALL ENOUGH TO BE HELD in one hand, this little box is made of wood and covered in leather, which is embossed with various designs including the Lamb of God holding a crucifix, two griffins and an ornate shield. Inside are three pewter bottles or jars known as *ampullae*, each inscribed with a letter or mark.

This set dates from around 1500 and was designed to hold the three oils blessed by a bishop on Holy Thursday, which were then used by a priest to administer important Catholic rites. One bottle is marked with three dots, probably representing the Holy Trinity. This would have held the chrism, a consecrated oil used especially in baptism. The bottle marked 'I' would have contained *oleum infirmorum*, the oil used for the sick. The third bottle would have held the oil of catechumens for Christian converts under instruction before baptism. Reserves of these sacred oils were kept in parish churches, but this portable box could have been carried by the priest serving his parishioners in their homes.

Once an essential part of Christian faith, the practice of using holy oils to transform the spiritual condition of individuals was not accepted by the Protestant faith and so most chrismatories were destroyed or repurposed after the Reformation. Holding on to such items signalled commitment to the old Roman Catholic faith, which was treated as subversive in threatening the security of the state. In Shakespeare's Stratford various items associated with Catholic worship were seized by the town Corporation in the wake of the Gunpowder Plot of 1605. A silver bell, an altar of stone, beads of amber and bone, and a pax (a small flat tablet inscribed with a sacred image) were confiscated by the organization.

Figure 1.3 A chrismatory designed to hold the three oils blessed by a bishop on Holy Thursday, 16th century, wood, leather and pewter, 9.7cm × 14cm × 6cm, SBT 1992-10.

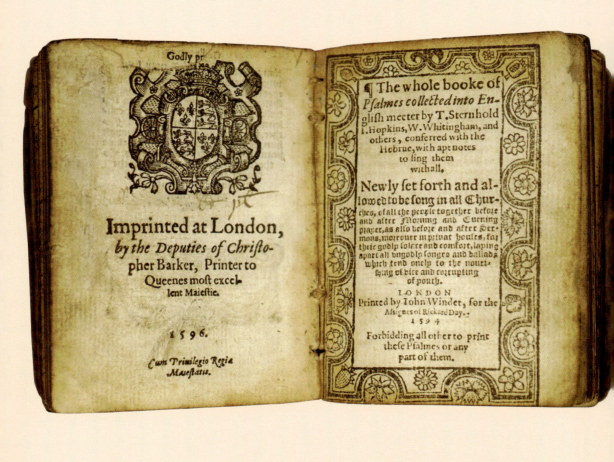

Godly pr

Imprinted at London,
by the Deputies of Christo-
pher Barker, Printer to
Queenes most excel-
lent Maiestie.

1596.

Cum Priuilegio Regiæ
Maiestatis.

¶ The whole booke of
Psalmes collected into English meeter by T. Sternhold
I. Hopkins, W. Whitingham, and
others, conferred with the
Hebrue, with apt notes
to sing them
withall.

Newly set forth and al-
lowed to be song in all Churches, of all the people together before
and after Morning and Euening
prayer, as also before and after Ser-
mons, moreouer in priuat houses, for
their godly solace and comfort, laying
apart all vngodly songes and ballads
which tend onely to the nouri-
shing of vice and corrupting
of youth.

LONDON
Printed by Iohn Windet, for the
Assignes of Richard Day.
1594

Forbidding all other to print
these Psalmes or any
part of them.

Book of Common Prayer
and Psalter

T HIS IS A COLLECTION OF texts bound together. The latest is a Psalter, or book of Psalms, which was printed in 1594. The cover is made of paper-pulp boards and is bound in leather. Some of this remains, but the spine has disappeared completely, revealing the sewed binding where the leaves have been gathered together. Its small size, roughly that of a mobile phone, meant that it could be carried around by the owner.

This book brings together three publications that formed a fundamental part of the English Protestant Church. Archbishop Cranmer's 1559 edition of the *Book of Common Prayer* is here, together with Archbishop Parker's *Thirty-Nine Articles of Religion* of 1563. This book also contains the *Whole Booke of Psalmes*, first published in 1594; a book that encouraged the communal singing of Psalms in church or, for the especially devout, in the home as well. Singing was restricted to the choir in Catholic services and so this book signalled an important shift towards the participation of the congregation in forms of Protestant worship.

This particular object is famous for its two 'Shakespearean' signatures: on the final page of the 'Confession of Fayth' can be seen an inked inscription, 'W Shakespear'; and opposite the first page of the Psalter there is a smudged signature: 'William Shakespear'. These scribbles, almost certainly forgeries of the late eighteenth or nineteenth century, are testament to Shakespeare's role in defining English religious identity – the forger here clearly wanted to claim Shakespeare as a Protestant poet.

Figure 1.4 'The boke of common praier, and administration of the sacramentes, and other rites and ceremonies in the Churche of Englande', Church of England, 1594, 9.5cm × 7.3cm × 5cm, London, SBT 83290001 (SR.98).

Corporation mace

B EARING THE INSIGNIA OF THE royal arms of England, this is a mace of the Corporation of Stratford-upon-Avon. It is mounted on a long shaft to be carried in ceremonial occasions. It dates from the fifteenth century and was modified later on, in the sixteenth century.

The most senior office-holder of a town in medieval and early modern England was duty bound, on the arrival of the monarch or monarch's representative to their region, to surrender the town's mace, whereupon the royal majesty would then kiss and return it. In performing this action, the relationship between the crown and the town was confirmed and demonstrated. The mace itself was a weapon, and as such it also symbolized the authority and power of local government to rule and punish wrongdoers.

This object was almost certainly handled by William Shakespeare's father, John, when he assumed the role of town Bailiff in 1568. Although he never met Elizabeth I, John would have walked behind the mace-bearer or Serjeant-at-Mace in official processions through the town, and this along with another mace (made around 1552) would almost certainly have been present at Corporation meetings, held regularly at 8.45 in the morning in the Guildhall on Church Street.

The mace was an instantly recognizable symbol of royal power in the hands of civic officials, and the ceremonies that helped reinforce that power is nowhere better described than in *Henry V*, 'O ceremony, show me but thy worth! / What is thy soul O adoration? / Art thou aught else but place, degree and form, / Creating awe and fear in other men?' (4.1.240–3).

Figure 1.5 Ceremonial mace, originally used by Stratford-upon-Avon's Guild of the Holy Cross, our Blessed Lady, and St John the Baptist, 1475–1550, English, silver and iron, 45cm, SBT 1868-3/1043.1.

Pike head

T HIS INCISED PEWTER PIKE HEAD, also known as a 'partizan', was made by a member of the Worshipful Company of Pewterers of London, and is inscribed with the date 1589. It shows a moustachioed soldier sporting a clipped beard and armed with pike and sword; he is dressed in billowing breeches and peascod doublet, with its characteristic overhanging belly. The pewter itself is thin and brittle indicating that this was a ceremonial pike rather than an actual weapon.

This 'partizan' was probably owned by a local civic body or Corporation, responsible for governing the towns of Shakespeare's England. Organizations like these orchestrated civic funerals, perambulations and parades, providing opportunities to display the importance of local officials and evoke the power of the monarch *in absentia*. The complex of Guild buildings in Stratford had an armoury with a number of 'pyks' used especially in the St George's Day celebrations throughout the sixteenth century.

The figure on this pike head, despite his portly demeanour, was for early modern viewers the paragon of male virility and bravery. The effect of the peascod and breeches were to draw attention to the wearer's sexual organs whilst also elongating the legs and arms, which displayed his athleticism. In addition, the man's facial hair, worn in a style known to contemporaries as the 'Roman T' beard, drew parallels not only with classical models of military valour, but with virile manhood itself – 'He that hath a beard is more than a youth' quips Beatrice in *Much Ado About Nothing*, 'and he that hath no beard is less than a man' (2.1.32–3). This object is one of many ways in which male identity, mixed with military and civic service, was performed in Shakespeare's time.

Figure 1.6 Filigree ceremonial spearhead, c.1580, English, pewter, 18cm × 9cm, SBT 1999-26.

Cloak clasp *no. 7*

T HIS IS A CLASP USED to pin a cloak together. It is made from pewter and brass and probably dates from the 1590s. It might originally have been gilded to look like gold. Cloaks were the outermost garment worn in Shakespeare's lifetime, much as we wear coats today. But cloaks were also a marker of status, worn in ceremonies and processions.

This clasp is particularly ornate and meaningful. It appears to have an image of Queen Elizabeth I set within a diamond-shaped frame, which in turn is surrounded by a crescent moon shape. The eight circular studs around the edge might signify the planets. Just discernible in the crescent's decoration are tiny flowers, possibly intended to represent the Tudor rose.

Later in her reign, Elizabeth was associated in art and poetry with the moon goddess Diana or Cynthia, because the moon controlled the tides. The Queen was celebrated as ruler over the seas and world, due to the maritime victories and exploration of this period. Sir Walter Raleigh fostered this association between Elizabeth and Cynthia to flatter the Queen but also to promote his vision of a global empire. She is depicted wearing moon-shaped jewels in several portraits between 1585 and 1600.

Elizabeth's courtiers wore small cameo portraits of the Queen as a sign of their loyalty, but as this object is made from relatively inexpensive materials it was affordable to civic officials, like John Shakespeare, who might have worn a clasp like this to demonstrate their commitment to Queen and state.

Figure 1.7 Decorated cloak clasp with the image of a richly dressed Elizabethan woman, c.1550s, English, pewter, 5.3cm (diam.), SBT 1997-19.

'Cubborde of Boxes'

T HIS LARGE CUPBOARD, STACKED WITH twelve drawers filled with numerous 'boxes' (four of which survive) has two panelled doors with heavy iron hinges and a pin-locking mechanism. It is a filing system; an early example of an attempt to organize and store official materials in a systematic way and it was at the heart of local government in Shakespeare's home town.

In the early sixteenth century important local documents were held by various organizations, including churches, manorial courts, guild premises, and even private individuals who had specific responsibilities such as clerks and stewards. Following the Reformation some towns were given rights and powers by royal charter to govern their own local affairs on behalf of the state. Stratford's royal charter was granted in 1553 and allowed the Corporation to make bye-laws, prosecute or present evidence against wrongdoers at the Court Leet, and receive a share of the fines exacted. This was part of a wider national impulse to coordinate and standardize local governmental practice, which in turn enabled other developments such as heightened information gathering, record keeping and improved methods of policing.

Due to the survival of a unique document in the Shakespeare Birthplace Trust collection, we know that this cupboard was made in sixteen and a half days by two local men, Lawrence Abell and Oliver Hiccox, and the finished cupboard was installed in the Guildhall Council Chamber in Stratford in 1595. As a 'filing cabinet' for the Corporation's records, including minute books, chamberlain's accounts, bye-laws, leases, as well as the maces, Chamber bible and prayerbook, the 'Cubborde of Boxes' represents the practical side of these organizational changes to daily civic business in the Stratford of Shakespeare's time.

Figure 1.8 Cupboard of Boxes made to hold the Stratford Corporation Records, English, 1594, oak, 186cm × 150cm, SBT L513.

Map of Warwickshire and Leicestershire

no. 9

P RODUCED IN 1576 *A Map of Warwickshire and Leicestershire* by Christopher Saxton is the first accurate representation of the county in which Shakespeare was born. It was commissioned by Lord Burghley, Queen Elizabeth's Chief Minister. From 1574 Saxton produced 35 coloured maps depicting the counties of England and Wales. Originally published as a collection in 1579, this volume was a landmark in British cartography. The map is engraved on a single copper-plate, with colour applied to pick out the main geographical features including water, vegetation, settlements and notable buildings. Rivers, streams, parks and woodlands are also depicted carefully. Despite some discrepancies Saxton's maps are impressively accurate and detailed. The importance and influence of the atlas he created is demonstrated by the fact that the maps were re-issued and adapted continually for almost two hundred years after their original appearance. For the first time these maps enabled people to gain a sense of their geographical location in relation to the country as a whole.

This map takes us to the heart of Shakespeare country, to the world in which Shakespeare was born and raised. It not only offers a view of Stratford, to the south of the large towns of Coventry and Warwick, but also provides a sense of a typical early modern rural English county. This is significant because Shakespeare placed many of his plays in rural or provincial settings. His experience of Warwickshire looms large in a number of his plays including *The Merry Wives of Windsor* which speaks of small-town life beyond the capital, and the Forest of Arden provides the mysterious setting for a number of scenes in *As You Like It*.

Figure 1.9 A map of Warwickshire and Leicestershire, by Christopher Saxton (c.1540–c.1610), 1576, printed on paper, 37cm × 50cm, SBT 1993-31/444.

Beeinge that heere after vvee intende to discribe euery thing in particular touchinge the parts of the vvorlde, vve vvill not heer vpon make any tedious circumstance, but onely touche a vvorde or tvvo, for the satisfaction and better light of the reader. In this mappe vve haue set the vvhole terrestiall globe, the vvhiche by the auncient vvriters vvas deuided into 3; partes, videlicet Europe, Asia, and Affrica, but sence this laste age our iounger Authours (vpon a further discouerye of almoste a nevve vvorlde) haue ioyned another parte therunto for the fourthe called America. Others more iounger haue adioyned a fifte parte, and call the same Magellana. Europe is encompassed rounde vvith vvater, except onlye vvhere it confineth vvith Asia, from the vvhiche it is separated by the riuer Tanais, dravvinge a lyne directlye from the originall or beginninge of the said ryuer, vntill the porte of S. Nicholas, beeinge in the norther sea, at this precient muche frequented by th'Englishe nations, the vvhiche make a greate trade there. Asia likevvise is enuironed by the sea, excepte the places vvhere it ioyneth vvith Europe aboue saide, and vvhere it is vnited vnto Affrica, by a straighte of lande, as is seene betvveene the redde and the Mediterranian sea, Iudea and Egipte, vvhere it is deuided and sundred. Africa shoulde be by it selfe, vvere it not ioyned as bouesside vnto Iudea, by the abouenamed straight of lande. Of America as yet there is no perfecte knovvledge vvhether it be an Ile, or elce, fastened vnto Asia tovvardes the north, yet there is good hope that the same may be fullie discouered by the good industrious diligence of the Englishe nation, vvho haue laboured muche about the same. Of the fifte parte of the earthe, vnder the meridian Pole, called Magellana or terra Australis, no matter of moment therof can be set dovvne, beeinge onlye yet discouered in but tvvoo or three places, videlicet, in the straight of Magellanes or terra del fuego, and in noua Ginnea, vvhiche is iudged to be a parte therof, as at large I vvill further relate. Antiquitie shevves that this vvhole globe of the earthe conteynes in her circumference fyue thovvsande and foure hundreth leagues, or 21600, Italian miles.

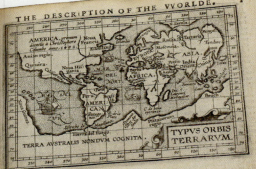

TYPVS ORBIS TERRARVM.

A

Pocket atlas

no. 10

THIS SMALL DARK LEATHER-BOUND book was printed in 1603. *Abraham Ortelius his epitome of the theatre of the worlde* is an abridged and smaller version of Ortelius' highly successful great atlas *Theatrum Orbis Terrarum* (*Theatre of the World*) published in 1570; the first geographical atlas in the modern sense. It measures 17cm by 13cm, roughly the size of a modern paperback novel, and contains 122 maps starting with a view of the World, Europe and including Africa, America, China and the Turkish Empire. Each map is accompanied by a brief historical and geographical description of the country providing information about the economic, cultural and social characteristics of the region depicted, including the lifestyle and manners of its inhabitants. The size and portability of this edition enabled more people to own such a volume for research, travel and general interest.

Ortelius' atlas provides us with a clear sense of the world as it was understood by Shakespeare and his contemporaries and speaks to the lasting contribution of sixteenth-century cartographers. While the English had always travelled in Europe, between 1578 and 1580 English sailors led by Francis Drake circumnavigated the world for the first time, fuelling a growing popular curiosity about foreign lands. Shakespeare's was an age of exploration, of cross-cultural trade and encounter. From Italy to Egypt and Arabia to Bermuda, Shakespeare used the entire world as the canvas for his work, and his fascination and desire to explore the globe at large is vividly expressed by Valentine in the opening scenes of *The Two Gentleman of Verona* – one of Shakespeare's earliest plays:

I rather would entreat thy company
To see the wonders of the world abroad
Than, living dully sluggardis'd at home

(1.1.5–7)

Figure 1.10 'Abraham Ortelius his epitome of the Theater of the worlde', or Pocket Atlas, 1603, by Abraham Ortelius (1527–98), London, 13cm × 17cm × 3.2cm. SBT 83081313 (SR 87).

21

Childhood 2

Painting of a Mother and Child   no. 11

T HIS PORTRAIT OF A MOTHER and child dates from around 1630 and is attributed to the Flemish painter, Cornelis de Vos (1584–1651) who specialized in similar family groups. The subjects are dressed in very fine clothing, with elaborate lace. The child is evidently teething; the ornate rattle at his side has at the end a curved piece of coral or bone for chewing and the mother offers what seems to be pieces of sugar, another hard substance great for gnawing as well as being an expensive luxury (sugar had not yet been identified with tooth decay).

The painting shows the custom of infant children wearing dresses in the sixteenth and seventeenth centuries, with no distinction between the sexes until a certain age. Once little boys were breeched, or put into trousers, a rite of passage that took place around the age of six or seven, they assumed their adult gender identity. While looking at his son Mamillius in *The Winter's Tale*, Leontes is reminded of the time when he too was 'unbreech'd, / In my green velvet coat' (1.2.155–6), worn by young petty-school charges. The practice of boys wearing dresses continued into the early twentieth century and can even be seen today in the traditional christening gown.

Though we do not know their identity, it is likely the father commissioned this painting to display pride in his family. It is evidence that the birth of a child was celebrated as a significant event worthy of commemoration. The painting marked an important rite of passage for the mother, too, in successfully producing an heir and surviving the ordeals and dangers of childbirth.

Figure 2.1 Painting of Mother and Child, possibly by Cornelis de Vos or Nicolaes Eliasz (Pickenoy), about 1630–35, oil on panel, 120cm × 87.5cm, SBT 1993-31/231.

Highchair *no. 12*

THIS ELABORATELY TURNED CHILD'S HIGHCHAIR dates from the period 1580 to 1640. It is Welsh, made of ash and is one of the finest extant examples of its kind. It survives in impeccable condition and, unlike most, still retains the original footboard. Its impressive turned decoration includes a crest of alternating pinnacles and buttons, and is supported by five uprights connected by eight reels with buttons and free rings. Such decoration must have served as a true tactile delight for tiny hands at the dinner table.

Turning as a form of furniture embellishment increased in popularity towards the end of the sixteenth century. A turner shaped the wood with a lathe (similar to a potter's wheel), which was powered by the pumping of a treadle, or lever, by the craftsman's foot.

Highchairs were probably pushed against the heavy tabletop, with their legs often splayed to increase stability. The chair's functionality suggests that toddlers took their meals at the same time as the rest of the family. Their proximity to the table, then, becomes important, as children were not set apart from the company of the meal, but ate alongside their elders.

Familial hierarchy was of utmost importance in Shakespeare's England, and meal times were a daily opportunity for the visual reinforcement of this household structure; a time of physical and spiritual nourishment. The inclusion of even the smallest members in this activity, as evidenced by highchairs, speaks to its significance.

Figure 2.2 Elaborately turned child's high chair, Welsh, 1580–1640, ash, 108cm × 48.5cm. SBT 1993–31/22.

Wooden doll *no. 13*

T HIS LITTLE CARVED WOODEN FIGURE is from the seventeenth century and may well be a child's doll. It is made from walnut and depicts a female figure with her hands clasped. She appears to wear some type of head covering and a dress that hits mid-calf with a necklace carved on her lower chest. She is bare foot with only four toes and stands at 22.8cm, supported by a block base.

Based on numerous portraits of children from the wealthiest families during Shakespeare's lifetime, it appears that boys and girls enjoyed playing with a wide range of toys including drums, hobby-horses and dolls. It is clear that children's desire to play was indulged and supported. There is some uncertainty as to whether this particular object was definitely a toy, but similar figures are identified with the so-called 'Bartholomew babies' sold at markets and the annual St Bartholomew fair (the word doll was not used in Shakespeare's time). These simple carved wooden figures could be dressed up in tiny pieces of clothing.

Philippe de Mornay's observation in his tract *A work concerning the trueness of the Christian Religion*, translated into English in 1587, suggests that toys were not uncommon at this time. He writes, 'how often hast thou taken from thy child a puppet or some other toy that he played withal, to see whether he would be stubborn or no . . . even when he cried to have it still?' It seems as though many of the children depicted in portraits, seen clutching earnestly to their dolls, may likewise have had such a reaction should someone have taken away their precious playthings.

Figure 2.3 Carved wooden doll, European?, 17th century, walnut, 22.8cm, SBT 1996-43.

Hornbook *no. 14*

T HE ITEM PICTURED HERE IS a seventeenth-century hornbook, made from wood, printed paper and ivory. Hornbooks were a key educational tool at this time, and were used to help children learn the basics of the English language. They would have been used in the home and at school, so the young Shakespeare would have handled an object like this. Hornbooks first appeared in England in the middle of the fifteenth century and were usually made of wood, leather or perhaps bone. Rectangular in shape, the handle at the bottom allowed easy grasping by small young hands. The face of each hornbook would have a sheet of vellum or paper pasted or tacked onto it, which would display the alphabet and in most cases also the Lord's Prayer, as in this example. This would then be protected by a thin layer of bone or horn, which is of course where the hornbook gets its name.

Unlike our teaching methods today, the children of Shakespeare's generation were not taught to read and write at the same time. Instead, being taught to read was the first priority, and they would use their hornbook as an aid to help them learn and memorise the alphabet and the Lord's Prayer. Only once they had learnt to read were they then taught the art of writing. Shakespeare makes reference to this act of learning in *Love's Labour's Lost*: 'Yes, yes! He teaches boys the hornbook. What is a, b, spelt backward with the horn on his head?' (5.1.44–5).

Figure 2.4 Hornbook, English, late 17th century, horn and wood, 11.1cm × 6cm, SBT 2008-1.

✝ A a b c d e f g h i j k l m n o p
r s t u v w x y z & ꜳ e i o u
A B C D E F G H I J K L M N O P
R S T U V W X Y Z

a e i o u · a e i o u
ab eb ib ob ub · ba be bi bo bu
ac ec ic oc uc · ca ce ci co cu
ad ed id od ud · da de di do du

In the Name of the Father, and of the
Son, and of the Holy Ghost. *Amen.*
OUR Father, which art in
Heaven, hallowed be thy
Name; thy Kingdom come; thy
Will be done on Earth, as it is in
Heaven. Give us this Day our
daily Bread; and forgive us our
Trespasses, as we forgive them
that trespass against us: And
lead us not into Temptation, but
deliver us from Evil. *Amen.*

The first Booke of Ouids

Metamorphosis, tranſlated into
Engliſh Meter.

F ſhapes transfoꝛmde to bodyes ſtrange,
    I purpoſe to intreate,
Ye Gods vouchſafe (foꝛ you are they,
    that wꝛought this wondꝛous feate)
To further this mine enterpꝛiſe.
    And from the woꝛld begunne,
Graunt that my Uerſe may to my time,
    his courſe directly runne.
Befoꝛe the Sea and Land were made, *Fab 1.*
    and Heauen, that all doth hide,
In all the woꝛlde one onely face of nature did abide,
Which Chaos hight, a huge rude heape, and nothing els but euen
A heauie lumpe and clottred clod of ſeedes together dꝛiuen,
Of things at ſtrife among themſelues, foꝛ want of oꝛder due.
No Sunne as yet with lightſome beames the ſhapeleſſe woꝛld did view,
No Moone in growing did repaire her hoꝛnes with boꝛowed light.
Noꝛ yet the earth amids the ayꝛe did hang by wondꝛous ſlight
Juſt peyſed by her pꝛoper weight. Noꝛ winding in and out
Did Amphitrytee with her armes embꝛace the earth about.
Foꝛ where was earth, was ſea and ayꝛe, ſo was the earth vnſtable,
The ayꝛe all darke, the ſea likewiſe to beare a ſhip vnable.
No kinde of thing had pꝛoper ſhape, but each confounded other.
Foꝛ in one ſelfe ſame body ſtroue, the hote and cold together.
The moyſt with dꝛy, the ſoft with hard, the light with things of weight.
This ſtrife did God and Nature bꝛeake, and ſet in oꝛder ſtreight.
The earth from heauen, the ſea from earth, he parted oꝛderly,
And from the thicke and foggy ayꝛe, he tooke the lightſome ſkie,
Which when he once vnfolded had, and ſeuered from the blinde
And clodded heape, He ſetting each from other did them binde
In endleſſe friendſhip to agree. The fire moſt pure and bꝛight,
The ſubſtance of the heauen it ſelfe, becauſe it was ſo light
Did mount aloft, and ſet it ſelfe in higheſt place of all.
The ſecond roome of right to ayꝛe, foꝛ lightneſſe did befall.

Ovid's Metamorphoses   *no. 15*

T**HIS BOOK IS AN EARLY** English edition of *Metamorphoses* by the Roman poet Ovid, translated by Arthur Golding in 1567. *Metamorphoses* is a Latin narrative poem which charts the history of the world from creation to the time of Julius Caesar; this great collection of myths and stories of the gods and heroes helped to shape the imagination of the ancient Roman world. This copy dates from 1603, and it is a beautiful example of early modern print.

Golding translated the ancient stories in a clear, faithful and vivid way which captivated his readers; his translation became highly influential and was certainly read by William Shakespeare and his contemporary, poet Edmund Spenser. Shakespeare would have first encountered the great Roman poets and prose writers of Virgil, Horace and Ovid in the upper classes of grammar school in Stratford-upon-Avon, and it is clear that this classical training and the books he read at school continued to influence him throughout his whole career. Shakespeare seems to have enjoyed Ovid's *Metamorphoses* the most, returning to it time and again as inspiration for his own work, including *Titus Andronicus*, based very clearly on the story of 'The Rape of Philomel' (indeed a copy of *Metamorphoses* appears on stage during the action, in Act 4 Scene 1), to *Romeo and Juliet* which draws upon the story of Pyramus and Thisbe, to Prospero's renunciation of his magic powers in *The Tempest* (taken from a speech by Medea in Book VII). Again in Sonnet 60, lines 1–2, Shakespeare's debt to Ovid is palpable in that both refer to the ebb and flow of time and life:

> Like as the waves make towards the pebbled shore,
> So do our minutes hasten to their end.

Figure 2.5 'The. XV. bookes of P. Ouidius Naso, entituled, Metamorphosis. Translated out of Latine into English meeter, by Arthur Golding, Gentle-man. A worke very pleasant and delectable.', 1603, by Ovid (43 BC–17 or 18 AD) and Arthur Golding (1536–1606) tr., London, 33cm × 22.8cm × 3.8cm, SBT 83000259 (SR 99.4).

The History of Four-Footed Beasts

*T*he *History of Four-Footed Beasts and Serpents* by Edward Topsell was printed in 1607 as the first comprehensive natural history book published in England. Based on an earlier volume by Conrad Gesner published in Zurich, it contains vivid descriptions and woodcut images of both real-life and mythological creatures. Running over 1,000 pages long, it is one of the most remarkable books held in the Shakespeare Birthplace Trust.

In the same way children tend to become fascinated by pets and dinosaurs today, these images of familiar and fantastical creatures must have captured the imagination of youngsters and adults alike. Topsell depicted many bizarre hybrid creatures like the hydra, a many-headed serpent, and the lamia, a scaly half-goat, half-bear, man-eater. The most sinister beast illustrated may well be the legendary manticore, a hairy creature with a lion's body and a man's head, bearing a tail full of piercing quills. Topsell outlines its ferocious attributes:

> This beast or rather monster ... having a treble row of teeth beneath and above ... his mouth reaching on both sides to his eares ... the tail of a scorpion of the earth, armed with a sting, casting forth sharp pointed quills ... his appetite is especially to the flesh of man.

Like Topsell, Shakespeare's works also appealed to a cultural fascination with monsters. In *The Tempest*, Caliban is styled as 'half a fish and half a monster' (3.2.29), and 'a freckled whelp hag-born, not honoured with a human shape' (1.2.283-4). When the play was performed in 1611, audiences who paid to see Caliban on stage may have been driven by the same interests as those who bought Topsell's book.

Figure 2.6 The 'Manticore' from *The History of Four-Footed Beasts and Serpents*, 1607, by Edward Topsell (1572–1625), London, 33.7cm × 23cm × 6.4cm, SBT 83080783 (SR OS 97).

Tortoise-shell box

THIS CURIOUS LITTLE TORTOISE-SHELL box evokes the early modern fascination with exotic and rare materials. In the seventeenth century, the shell was fitted with decorated silver clasps, transforming the two shell halves into a unique lockable box roughly the size of a half-dozen carton of eggs.

The distinctive brown and orange radiating pattern that decorates the shell identifies it as once belonging to a Star Tortoise, originating from either India or Sri Lanka. The shine of the tortoise's scales makes the container gleam with a deep richness and gives it a textured finish. Emptied of its keepsake, we can only speculate about the precious items the box may have originally held and protected – perhaps costly jewellery or a small, cherished trinket from a loved one. Whatever its use, the exotic nature of the box suggests it held similarly impressive and whimsical items.

Tortoise shells regularly featured in 'cabinets of curiosities', also known as 'wonder rooms', which were collections of extraordinary natural and man-made objects and rarities, such as narwhale tusks, astrological manuscripts and dodo birds. Shakespeare includes a tortoise shell in the apothecary's shop (another kind of wonder room) in *Romeo and Juliet*, 'And in his needy shop a tortoise hung, / An alligator stuff'd, and other skins / Of ill-shaped fishes' (5.1.42–4). Like cabinets of curiosities, the little tortoise-shell box is an expression of the authority of man over nature: the natural beauty and interest of the patterned shell has been augmented by the addition of silver hinges and clips, converting it into someone's personal – and presumably prized – possession.

Figure 2.7 Indian star tortoise shell with 17th-century European silver mounts, shell and silver, 7.1cm × 11.6cm × 8.4cm, SBT 2006-34.

Youth 3

Gloves

T HIS PAIR OF MEN'S GLOVES dates from the seventeenth century. They are made of high quality kid leather and are lined with pink silk. They are also lavishly decorated, with silver bullion braid and floral designs embroidered on the cuffs.

Shakespeare's father John was a glover and whittawer (leather worker) by trade, so the young playwright would have grown up being familiar with how gloves were made and sold. These gloves are, however, a far remove from the staple wares produced by his father. The quality of the materials and the extent of the decoration make it clear that the main function of these gloves was not to keep their wearer's hands warm. Gloves in early modern times also served an important function as markers of social status: this pair would have been owned by a man who wanted to display his substantial wealth and social standing. Gloves could also be displayed by being carried or tucked into a hat band. They are often held, rather than worn, in portraits of the time.

Gloves were also a popular gift given during courtship at this time. The act of gift-giving during courtship demonstrated the man's honourable intentions to his beloved; the woman's acceptance of the gift indicated her happiness and commitment to the relationship. Shakespeare makes reference to these practices in his play, *The Winter's Tale*, where the shepherdess Mopsa says to her sweetheart: 'Come, you promised me a tawdry-lace and a pair of sweet gloves' (4.4.250–1).

Figure 3.1 Pair of men's kid gloves, 1600s, kid leather, silk and silver, 35cm × 11cm, SBT 1992-2.

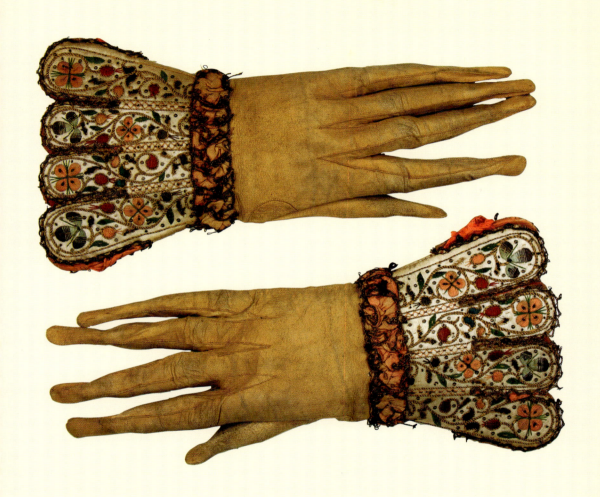

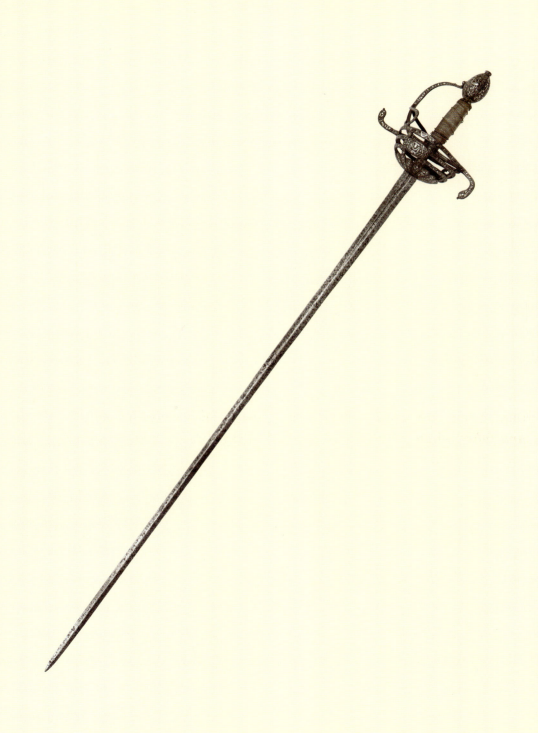

Sword   *no. 19*

T HIS IS A CERTAIN KIND of sword, known as a rapier. Swords were worn as a sign of status and martial ability by gentlemen. This rapier has a cupped or shell guard and an oviform pommel encrusted with decorative silver Kuffic script, which was extremely fashionable in the early seventeeth century. This exotic motif doubled as a signifier of quality – the best swords were thought to come from Spanish 'Catalan forges' and the Moorish craft tradition. Whilst the maker's mark struck on both sides of the blade is illegible, this item was almost certainly made in Spain, around 1600.

From the 1540s to the time of Shakespeare's death, the rapier was the epitome of sophistication – elaborately decorated, easily slung from the belt, quickly drawn and perfectly designed for rapid long-range thrusting. Having these weapons on hand, however, encouraged ready duelling by hot-blooded young men in response to the slightest quarrel. Shakespeare plunges into the world of Renaissance youth and deadly swagger in *Romeo and Juliet*, where gentility and masculinity are defined by swordplay. Men were expected to duel to defend their honour, although many early modern writers suggest that participants were more concerned with proving their virility and prowess than defending valiantly a moral cause.

Other more reactionary writers commented that rapiers were 'fantasticall', alluring and cosmopolitan, yet 'weake' and, by implication, effeminate. By the seventeenth century however, rapiers had become key pieces of fashion, and an opportunity for men to display their taste and style as well as status.

Figure 3.2 Swept-hilt rapier, England, c.1610, silver, 96cm, SBT 1993-28.

Bodice no. 20

THIS HIGHLY-EMBELLISHED ITEM OF clothing dates to around 1610, and this type of garment would have been known to Shakespeare and his contemporaries as 'bodies' or a 'pair of bodies'. What we wear as a single 'bodice' today would, in Shakespeare's time, have been worn as two separate pieces of material, one for the front and one for the back of the body (hence the name). These pieces would have been laced into place each day. The sleeves would also have been attached separately, although the sleeves on this garment have been stitched on, probably at a later date. This pair of bodies is made of fine linen and is elaborately and beautifully embroidered: the yellow and green leaf pattern retains its vibrancy, while the gold stitching detail still sparkles. A closer look, however, reveals that the decoration was not quite completed on the back panel and edging.

As described in relation to the gloves and sword, clothing and accessories in Shakespeare's time were a very important means of displaying wealth and status; the fine linen and beautiful embroidery of this garment means that only a lady of some wealth and standing would have been able to afford such an expensive item. In *Antony and Cleopatra*, Shakespeare apparently imagines the Egyptian queen in clothing that would have been familiar to his audience. Cleopatra pretends to be ill and begs to be cut out of her dress, taking advantage of the known effects of tight lacing to try and prevent Antony's departure:

> Cut my lace, Charmian, come!
> But let it be; I am quickly ill, and well –
> So Antony loves.
>
> (1.3.72–4)

Figure 3.3 Elaborately embroidered bodice, c.1610, English, linen, silk and silver, 35cm × 51cm (arm) × 31cm (shoulder), SBT 1993-35.

Thimble

THIS LITTLE SILVER THIMBLE DATES from the early seventeenth century. Thimbles are, of course, worn during sewing to protect the finger that pushes the needle through the fabric. This object, however, has decoration that indicates it has a symbolic role as well as a practical function. It is engraved with two flower heads and two crosses on a 'waffle' pattern ground. Around the border at the base are engraved the words 'Be Trw In Love As Tvrtl Dove' and on the top are the initials ME. This decoration reflects how thimbles were associated with the rituals of courtship in Tudor England. The posy on this thimble speaks of the faithful nature of the turtle dove which was recognised as a symbol of true love in this period, as Shakespeare himself articulates in his enigmatic poem, 'The Phoenix and the Turtle'. Other common gifts given during courtship include gloves and handkerchiefs; however a thimble had a further powerful symbolic meaning. Representing the domestic role of women, the gift of a thimble would have carried the man's expectations of his future wife. This symbolism was not lost on Shakespeare who makes reference to the thimble as an object of female domesticity in his play *King John* with Philip the Bastard's speech:

And you degenerate, you ingrate revolts,
            . . . blush for shame:
For your own ladies and pale-visag'd maids
Like Amazons come tripping after drums,
Their thimbles into armed gauntlets change,
Their needl's to lances, and their gentle hearts
To fierce and bloody inclination.
                  (5.2.151–8)

Figure 3.4 Silver thimble engraved with legend 'Be Trw In Love As Tvrtl Dove', 1600s, English, silver, 2.9cm, SBT 1995-38.

Sweet bag

T HIS LATE SIXTEENTH-CENTURY 'sweet bag', despite its name, was actually not a bag for sweets at all. In fact, it was a kind of purse which might have had a variety of possible uses. It also looks remarkably like the sort of thing Shakespeare may have had in mind when writing this speech from *Troilus and Cressida*, in which Thersites unleashes his anger at Patroclus:

> Why art thou then exasperate, thou idle immaterial skein of sleave-silk, thou green sarsenet flap for a sore eye, thou tassel of a prodigal's purse, thou? Ah, how the poor world is pestered with such waterflies, diminutives of nature!
>
> (5.1.29–33)

This purse is also made of silk (specifically, silk satin), except in this case it is dark pink instead of green. Sarcenet was a silk-like material and so only available to the wealthier citizens of Shakespeare's England. It is embroidered with foliage detail in yellows and greens which are still vibrant today, with silver spangles enhancing the border and background. It too is edged with tassels, two of which are acorn-shaped. A long, seven-colour plaited drawstring and cord is attached to the top, which perhaps allowed for the bag to be carried around the wrist or hung about the person, for maximum display.

Bags like these were often used to hold gifts of money presented to the monarch at New Year, as a kind of early modern gift wrapping. A gorgeous bag like this might even have been given as a token of love during court-ship, perhaps containing a smaller, symbolic gift within, like a ring, or like the thimble featured above.

Figure 3.5 Embroidered sweet bag, silk, gold and silver, 11cm × 32.5cm × 25cm, SBT 1992-86.

Marriage and Domestic Life

4

Painted cloth *no. 23*

T HIS IS A DETAIL OF one of three pieces of painted wall hanging dating from the late seventeenth or early eighteenth century. It is a rare and precious survival of an art form that was common in domestic houses in Shakespeare's lifetime. Together these hangings illustrate the biblical story of the marriage of Isaac and Rebecca (Genesis 24). The scene shown here of figures and camels at a well can be identified as Eliezer (Isaac's servant) courting Rebecca on Isaac's behalf. The theme of a felicitous marriage would have been particularly appropriate for display in the home and might have been given or purchased to commemorate the founding of a household. The size of this section of textile (11ft by 7ft) gives some impression of the impact of this expansive wall decoration, which served to insulate as well as adorn domestic space. William Harrison in his *Description of England* (1577) explained the effect of such hangings in making rooms, 'not a little commended, made warm, and much more close than otherwise they would be'.

Shakespeare's familiarity with painted cloths is evident in several of his plays; he alludes to the wise proverbial texts written on cloths but also evokes the range of imagery that could be seen. In *Henry IV, Part I* Falstaff refers to another biblical subject – the parable of the Rich Man and Lazarus: 'my whole charge consists of ensigns, corporals, lieutenants, gentleman of companies – slaves as ragged as Lazarus in the painted cloth, where the glutton's dogs licked his sores' (4.2.23–6). In *Love's Labour's Lost* Sir Nathaniel's poor performance in a masque of the Nine Worthies (a group of ancient heroes popular in pageantry and visual art) prompts Costard to tease: 'O sir, you have overthrown Alisander the conqueror. You will be scraped out of the painted cloth for this' (5.2.570–2).

Figure 4.1 Painted wall hanging showing four muses at a well, late 17th century, canvas or linen, 335cm × 232cm, SBT 1993-63/3.

Carved knife sheath   *no. 24*

T HIS WOODEN SHEATH WAS CARVED in 1602 by a Flemish craftsman known only by his initials, W.G.W. It would have contained two items of cutlery (now lost), and its exterior is carved with scenes from the Prodigal Son from the Gospel of Luke (15: 11–32). On the opposite side are six illustrations of the Works of Mercy, works of charity based on Christ's teachings. W.G.W.'s workshop produced various cases for clients all over Europe. Over fifteen examples of his work are in British collections alone. This is a particularly fine example with extensive and accomplished craftsmanship.

During Shakespeare's time it was usual for people of the upper and middling sort to carry around their own cutlery. Most people would own at least one knife; less common were complete sets of knife, fork and tooth-picks. This object was part of a wider early modern category of 'girdle furniture' in which possessions suspended from the belt could communicate different ideas, values or desires. Pairs of knives were commonly given as wedding tokens, either for the bride to wear, or to commemorate the betrothal. Scandinavian and Dutch folk custom suggests that an empty sheath, like this, worn by a virgin was a sign of her readiness to marry, and this may have influenced English customs. In fact the language of cutlery in England was also saturated in sexual connotations; in *Romeo and Juliet*, 'lay[ing the] knife aboard' suggested a male sexual advance (2.4.199–200), whilst King Lear describes female upper thighs and buttocks as 'forks' (4.6.117).

Figure 4.2 Carved sheath for a pair of knives, 1602, Dutch, boxwood, 23cm, SBT 1868-3/903.

Wooden chest *no. 25*

Tʜɪs ʜᴀɴᴅsᴏᴍᴇ ᴏᴀᴋ cʜᴇsᴛ dates to around 1575 and is carved with figures from classical and biblical mythology. Amongst others, it features Lucretia, and Judith with the head of Holofernes. Lucretia's rape and subsequent suicide was thought to have sparked the creation of the Roman Republic. The story of Judith and Holofernes is found in the Old Testament Book of Judith; Judith seduces and then beheads the drunken Holofernes in order to prevent his army's invasion of her city. This particular chest is French, but examples like this would have been a familiar sight in most early modern English homes too, although the quality of wood and decoration would have varied according to social status and wealth.

Chests were often associated with women, marriage and good housekeeping. In *The Taming of the Shrew*, Gremio itemises the contents of his chest in an attempt to win the hand of Bianca:

> In cypress chests my arras counterpoints,
> Costly apparel, tents and canopies,
> Fine linen, Turkey cushions boss'd with pearl,
> Valance of Venice gold in needlework,
> Pewter and brass, and all things that belongs
> To house or housekeeping.
>
> (2.1.345–50)

Chests could also contain the essential items, like linens and bedclothes, that a woman would bring to her new home. As a storage place for valuables, chests like this would commonly be found in chambers at the foot of the bed. Shakespeare draws out the symbolic association of these objects with female fidelity in *Cymbeline* (Act 2 Scene 2) when Iachimo hides in a chest in Imogen's chamber later to emerge and spy on her in her sleep. It is a literal violation of her personal space, which allows Iachimo plausibly to question her chastity.

Figure 4.3 Chest carved with figures from classical mythology, c.1570, French, oak, 111cm × 55cm × 76cm, SBT 1993-31/268.

The 'Hathaway Bed'   *no. 26*

ONE OF THE MOST EXPENSIVE items in early modern households of the elite and middling sort was the tester bedstead. This impressive oak, four poster bedstead is English and dates from the sixteenth and seventeenth centuries. It is made up of parts from different periods; the tester (canopy) dates from around 1650 while the headboard, posts and rails date from 1580 to 1630. Traditionally known as the 'Hathaway Bed', it was purchased by the Shakespeare Birthplace Trust in 1892 along with Anne Hathaway's Cottage itself, and it is thought to have been *in situ* there for many years prior to this. Shakespeare's wife, Anne, lived at the cottage as a child and the house remained in the Hathaway family for several generations.

Tester beds were a symbol of wealth and status, and were often acquired on the occasion of a marriage to be first used by the couple on their wedding night. This bedstead is decorated in the fashionable Flemish style. Elaborate carving on the headboard includes hybrid human and animal figures known as caryatids and atlantes, and the bedposts and tester are covered with carved flowers and geometric designs. This kind of imagery was associated with fertility and regeneration, and might serve to symbolize the three major rites of passage – birth, marriage and death – each of which took place in beds. As it was not uncommon for multiple people to sleep in a room, whether on the floor or on smaller truckle beds, which rolled out from under the main bed, tester bedsteads were hung round with curtains. These were for warmth, as well as privacy, and were often woven with rich colours and fabrics, perhaps with images of flora and fauna, creating a simulated 'flowery bed' (*A Midsummer Night's Dream*).

Figure 4.4 Tester bed, known as the 'Hathaway Bed', late 16th century–17th century, English, oak, 211cm × 200cm × 156cm, SBT 1993-31/648.

Long cushion cover   no. 27

THIS HIGH-QUALITY TAPESTRY CUSHION cover is an example of a popular form of domestic interior decoration in the homes of the elite and middling sorts. Dating from around 1600 it was probably made by Flemish craftsmen working in London and was an expensive item, which would have been for display, rather than for physical comfort; there is little sign of wear and tear – in fact it is in excellent condition. But its lively imagery could entertain while serving to maintain order and moral discipline in the household. It depicts three scenes from the biblical story of Joseph (Genesis 37–46) and additional shorter cushions may once have extended and completed the narrative.

In Shakespeare's England, adultery was considered one of the greatest threats to marriage and social order. The scene depicted in the cushion's central section is the attempted seduction of Joseph by Potiphar's wife, which warns against this particular sin. Wrapped half-naked in a sheet in front of a richly dressed bed adorned with curtains, presumably made of silk, and a runner of golden tassels, the adulteress grabs hold of Joseph's cloak with one hand as he tries to escape, and with the other beckons him to join her on the bed.

The cushion was probably displayed on a window bay or bed where potentially flirtatious conversation could take place. Many religious images were removed from churches throughout England around the time of Shakespeare's birth, but it was common to use biblical imagery in domestic interiors after the Reformation where it served to instruct, remind, encourage and – in this case – warn its viewers.

Figure 4.5 Tapestry panel depicting the biblical story of Joseph, English, 16th century, 99cm × 55cm, SBT 1993-31/299.

An allegorical painting   no. 28

THIS PAINTING IS AN ALLEGORY, apparently combining the biblical story of Susanna and the Elders with the theme of 'Touch', one of the Five Senses. It is attributed to the school of the Netherlandish artist Frans Floris the Elder and dates from around 1550.

The story of Susanna tells how a beautiful wife was bathing in her garden and was spied upon by two town elders. They desired her and threatened to accuse her of adultery if she would not sleep with them. When she refused the elders lied to have her condemned to death but the boy prophet Daniel saw the truth of the matter and the elders were executed instead. The theme of chastity is picked up in the symbolic glass and pearls on the stone seat next to the female figure; a glass was often used as a sign of fragility or transience, while the pearls were a common symbol of purity.

The clue to the theme of touch is the little tortoise spouting water perched on the wall above the figures. The Five Senses were often depicted in Renaissance art as women in classical drapery with animals symbolic of their particular Sense; the tortoise represented Touch.

The moral of this visual story, therefore, seems to be to avoid elicit touching. In *Cymbeline* Act 2, Scene 2, when Iachimo spies on Imogen in her bed he is filled with desire: 'That I might touch! But kiss, one kiss!' (2.2.16–17). Like Imogen, Susanna provided an example of chastity and fortitude in resisting the amorous advances of men. The didactic message of this painting served as a reminder of the need to behave with virtue and piety, rather than indulging bodily senses.

Figure 4.6 Painting depicting the allegory of Susanna and the Elders, c.1550, attributed to the school of Frans Floris the Elder (1517–70), 57cm × 44cm, SBT 1993-31/315.

Painting of a kitchen scene   no. 29

T HIS OIL PAINTING ON WOODEN panel is associated with the workshop of Joachim Beukelaer (1530–73), but was probably painted in the early part of the seventeenth century by another artist influenced by his work. It presents a feast for the eyes and stomach: game, fish, offal and meat such as rabbits, hare, swan, pike, trout, suckling pig, partridge, pigeons, mallards, turkey, a skinned cow head on a butcher's block, and an assortment of vegetables and fruits crowd the surface of the picture. A 'maid' plucks a goose in the top right, whilst the illusionistic *trompe l'oeil* effect is striking in the top left: a piece of paper, seemingly hammered into the panel, reads 'I have choice for my kitchen'.

The point of this painting was perhaps to arouse the appetite of the viewer – we could imagine this picture hanging in a tavern and drooled over by customers – as well as celebrating the wealth, status and productivity of the domestic economy that could furnish such a wonderful spread. For this reason, it is also possible that this picture might have hung in a private home.

In the late sixteenth and seventeenth centuries, the living standards of the middling ranks of society rose steeply, and people were able and inclined to entertain friends in their own homes rather than in public houses. There were a variety of innovations; improved fireplaces, staircases, furnishings for entertainment, as well as new eating and drinking cultures with their own codified rules, games, songs and objects. A painting like this would have suited the pretensions and prosperity of Shakespeare's own grand home, New Place in Stratford-upon-Avon, which he bought, and possibly renovated, in 1597.

Figure 4.7 'Game, Poultry, Fish and Vegetables with a Maid Plucking a Goose', 1601–33, unknown artist of Anglo-Dutch School, oil on board, 63.5cm × 93.5cm, SBT 2006-29.

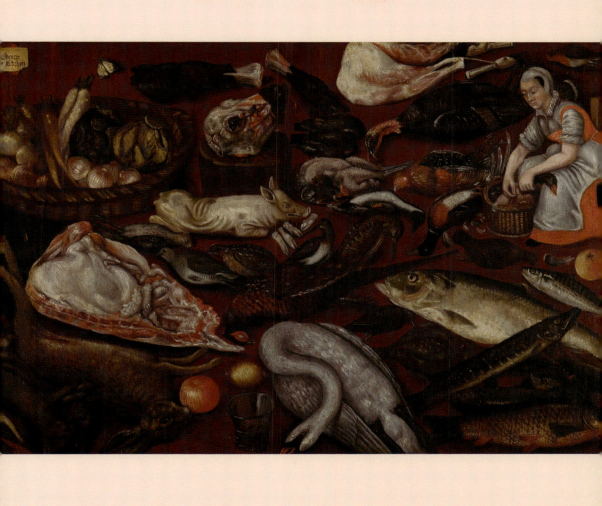

Painting of 'A Family Saying Grace Before A Meal'

no. 30

FROM KITCHEN TO TABLE – in this painting by Flemish artist Anthonius Claeissins, a wealthy family gathers around a dining table. The meal remains untouched as each family member holds their hands in prayer, giving thanks to God before eating. Husband and wife are given primary importance seated in the middle of the table, their children arranged in descending order of age around them. The table is laid with a fine damask tablecloth and is laden with pewter plates, a silver cup and a pair of silver-gilt salt-cellars.

This portrait reflects the importance assigned to mealtimes in family and religious life in the sixteenth century. Families were thought of as 'little churches' as the household was the daily focus for pious service to God, with carefully outlined responsibilities for husband and wife. These are represented, quite cleverly, through the open window behind the family: a single tree stands by a river and a vine grows against a wall. The tree alludes to the father's duty to serve as a family man, as referred to in Psalm 1: 'And he shall be like a tree planted by the rivers of water, that bringeth forth his fruit in his season.' Psalm 128 figures a wife as a fruiting vine, responsible for bringing forth children: 'Thou wife shall be as a fruitful vine by the sides of thine house: thy children like olive plants about thy table.' Shakespeare draws on this theme in his play, *The Comedy of Errors*, when Adriana addresses a man she thinks is her husband:

> Thou art an elm, my husband; I a vine,
> Whose weakness married to thy stronger state,
> Makes me with thy strength to communicate
>
> (2.2.173–5)

Figure 4.8 'A Family Saying Grace Before A Meal', c.1580, Anthonius Claeissins (1538–1613), oil on board, 142cm × 96.5cm, SBT 1990-49.

Cauldron

STAYING WITH THE THEME OF cooking and eating, this is a cauldron dating from the late fifteenth to early sixteenth century and is made of bronze. It has two handles (or 'lugs') near the rim, to allow it to be suspended over a fire to boil or stew its contents. This particular cauldron also has three feet on the bottom, which means it could also have stood directly on the hearth for cooking. Cauldrons were commonplace domestic items during Shakespeare's lifetime, and were used by the women of the household for cooking meals for the family. They were therefore bound up with the idea of female domesticity at this time, and Shakespeare subverts the ideal image of housewives to great effect in his portrayal of the three witches in *Macbeth*:

> Double, double, toil and trouble:
> Fire, burn; and cauldron, bubble . . .
> Fillet of a fenny snake,
> In the cauldron boil and bake;
> Eye of newt, and toe of frog,
> Wool of bat and tongue of dog . . .
> For a charm of powerful trouble,
> Like a hell-broth boil and bubble.
> (4.1.10–19)

These women are not providing for their families by cooking food in the cauldron, as they should do; they are instead using it to brew evil potions. The detail Shakespeare includes about the sorts of gruesome 'ingredients' the witches use makes plain their corruption of ordinary food preparation, and that they are to be feared. The image of the witches with their cauldron is so powerful that it has become the archetypal representation of witches: even in movies today any witch worth her salt will have an enormous cauldron adorning her lair.

Figure 4.9 Cauldron or cooking pot, 17th century, bronze (copper alloy), 13cm × 20.5cm, SBT 1995-6.

Joint-stool

'JOINT-STOOLS' WERE ONE OF the most common pieces of furniture in early modern households. This example is one of a pair dating from the first half of the seventeenth century and is a more ornate version of the standard type, with turned legs and curved decorative panels under the seat. These sturdy but lightweight seats of simple construction were easily transportable and relatively cheap, and even served as useful stage props in the theatre. But the humble joint-stool may also have triggered associations with magic and folklore for Shakespeare's audience!

In popular belief it was thought that witches had the ability to enchant certain ordinary domestic objects, such as stools, to take on their appearance. During Issobell Gowdie's 1662 trial for witchcraft in Scotland, recorded in a compilation of *Ancient Criminal Trials*, the housewife admitted in detail to many of the alleged practices of witches, claiming they placed brooms or stools beside their husbands in bed and repeated this spell three times: 'I lay down this broom [or stool], in the Devil's name, let it not stir until I come again'. Immediately the object would take on the appearance of the wife beside her husband so she could go unnoticed about her business.

Though the Fool in *King Lear* apologizes to Goneril for mistaking her for one such item, 'Cry you mercy, I took you for a joint-stool' (3.6.51) possibly in an attempt to slight her, it may also have been his way of calling her a witch! Lady Macbeth's exasperation at her husband's crazy behaviour likewise alludes to these superstitious associations. Indeed, though she believes her husband looks 'but on a stool' (3.4.67), Macbeth sees something altogether different – the ghost of Banquo!

Figure 4.10 One of a pair of joint-stools, c.1630, oak, 57cm × 44.5cm × 25cm, SBT 2005-35/2 & 3.

'Bartmann' jug

T HIS BROWN STONEWARE VESSEL IS known as a 'Bartmann jug' (*Bartmann* being the German word for 'bearded man'). Its name derives from its most distinguishing feature, a bearded face which decorates the neck and rounded body of the jug. These jugs were widely imported from Germany and have been found in archaeological sites around the world. Hundreds of examples have been found in England where they were used for storing and transporting food and drink and decanting wine. They would have been a common sight on the dining table.

However, the most fascinating use of these jugs was in their occasional transformation into a 'witch bottle', a vessel which protected against witchcraft by drawing in spells cast against its owner and entrapping them within the bottle, effectively tormenting the witch who cast it. To activate the charm, it was filled with its owner's bodily matter, which could include hair, fingernail clippings and human urine. The bottle was then sealed with a cork and hidden within the home, usually under a door threshold or buried below the central hearth (probably to keep the urine warm). This meant it worked as a natural substitute for the owner, but it was also thought to affect the witch's ability to urinate, causing him or her severe pain. Bartmann jugs may have been selected for this purpose because of the malevolent-looking bearded face as well as their bladder-shaped form.

Although these jugs were relatively common objects used for everyday purposes of storing and transporting goods, the conversion of such items into charms is evidence of cultural anxiety surrounding the power of witches to inflict harm, cause illness, accident and injury and disrupt the daily life of the household.

Figure 4.11 Bartmannkrug, 1601–25, German, stoneware, height 20cm, SBT 2004-50/1.

Professional Life 5

View of London Bridge   *no. 34*

FOR MANY PEOPLE IN Elizabethan England, the path to a successful career led to London. Shakespeare seems to have established his family life in Stratford before pursuing his professional life in London, but most people would have established their trade before getting married and raising children.

This engraving of 1597 by John Norden depicts a view of London Bridge and is one of the best representations of the city during this period; it is rather wonderful in its detail. On the right is a panel describing the bridge; here we discover that 102 homes are built along and over the 30-foot-wide road into the city. On the river are small rowing boats or 'taxi-boats' – the most common method of crossing the river. On the right is an overturned boat, the oars floating and a man drowning, while two others are being saved. At the south end (left) is the gate, above which are the heads of executed criminals on spikes.

This is the bustling city Shakespeare would have encountered on his arrival to find a job in the theatre. Many Londoners were strict Protestants who objected to the theatres and the bawdy nature of some plays, as well as the fighting and drinking which often accompanied them. The theatres were forced out to the suburbs and many were in Southwark on the south bank of the River Thames; this was the only bridge across it. Passing under the gatehouse – with its severed heads – to the theatre, where the political and social issues of the day were played out, must have provided a sharp reminder that traitors would not be tolerated.

Figure 5.1 'The view of London Bridge from east to weste', 1597, by John Norden (1548–1625), print on paper, 38.9cm × 52.2cm, SBT 83271406 (SR OS 87.7).

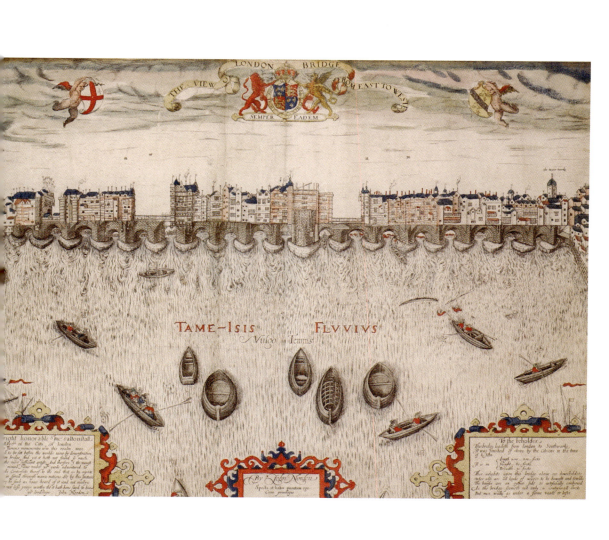

Hard fauourd tyrant, ugly, meagre, leane,
Hatefull diuorce of loue, (thus chides fhe death)
Grim-grinning ghoft, earths-worme what doft thou
To ftifle beautie, and to fteale his breath? (meane?
   VVho when he liu'd, his breath and beautie fet
   Gloffe on the rofe, fmell to the violet.

Ifhe be dead, ô no, it cannot be,
Seeing his beautie, thou fhouldft ftrike at it,
Oh yes, it may, thou haft no eyes to fee,
But hatefully at randon doeft thou hit,
   Thy marke is feeble age, but thy falfe dart,
   Miftakes that aime, and cleaues an infants hart.

Hadft thou but bid beware, then he had fpoke,
And hearing him, thy power had loft his power,
The deftinies will curfe thee for this ftroke,
They bid thee crop a weed, thou pluckft a flower,
   Loues golden arrow at him fhould haue fled,
   And not deaths ebon dart to ftrike him dead.

Doeft thou drink tears, that thou prouok'ft fuch wee-
VVhat may a heauie grone aduantage thee? (ping,
VVhy haft thou caft into eternall fleeping,
Thofe eyes that taught all other eyes to fee?
   Now nature cares not for thy mortall vigour,
   Since her beft worke is ruin'd with thy rigour.

Venus and Adonis *no. 35*

THIS SINGLE SHEET OF PAPER is an extremely rare survival. It is a loose leaf from the poem *Venus and Adonis*. Many will be surprised to discover that Shakespeare's first, and one of his most popular, published works was not a play but an epic poem inspired by a Roman poet. The story of *Venus and Adonis* is taken from Book 10 of Ovid's *Metamorphoses*, where Venus the goddess of love falls deeply in love with a human, the young hunter Adonis who dies after being attacked by a boar in a tragic accident. In Ovid's version Adonis is a willing lover, while Shakespeare twists the tale so that Adonis resists Venus; showing off his poetic but also his comedic skills.

Written during a period when the London theatres were frequently closed due to the plague, *Venus and Adonis* was a huge success, indeed, it was the most popular poem of the Elizabethan age; read by many and quoted in poetry and prose of the day. It was first published and printed in quarto format by Shakespeare's fellow townsman Richard Field, and due to its popularity was printed again and again; and yet of a thousand original copies produced only one full copy of that first edition survives. This single loose page comes from a rare second quarto edition of 1594. It is from towards the end of the poem and contains the lines 907–54, here we read the moment when Venus sees the boar's mouth covered in blood and wonders if Adonis is dead.

When in 1594, the plague abated and the theatres reopened, Shakespeare returned to writing for the stage employing his skills of crafting poetry to the great pleasure of his audiences.

Figure 5.2 'Venus and Adonis', 1594, William Shakespeare (1564–1616), single page of paper, 18.4cm × 12.2cm, SBT 83000070 (SRP.35.44).

Money box

THIS CERAMIC, GREEN-GLAZED POT dates to between 1550 and 1650. It has a large, bulbous body, a tapering top with distinctive 'knob' detail, and a slit in its side. These features indicate that it was used as a money box. Boxes like these would have been used to collect money as people went to see the latest play in London's first theatres. (In fact, it is thought that the office in which these boxes would have been stored may be where our term 'box office' originates). People called 'gatherers' would have been located, holding these boxes, at entrance points around the theatre, and theatregoers would pay a penny to stand and see the play as a 'groundling'. If they preferred to sit, they could pay further pennies as they moved up into the galleries. One of the distinctive features of this form of money box is that it is entirely sealed: there is no opening to allow for the removal of the money from within. In order to retrieve the contents, the jar has to be smashed. In the world of Shakespeare's theatres, these money boxes were not intended to be durable, financially valuable objects in themselves, but instead were used because they were sturdy, portable and cheap. This made them ideally suited for collecting large quantities of cash in a short amount of time. As a result of their brief lives and destructive ends, survivals of complete examples are rare. This one looks complete, but it actually has a hole in the base which was probably made by an owner retrieving its contents.

Figure 5.3 Elizabethan money pot, 1550–1650, English, earthenware, 10cm × 8.5cm (max. diam.), SBT 1996-28.

Wee Three Loᵍᵉʳʰᵈˢ

Painting of 'Wee Three Loggerheads'   no. 37

WHEN YOU LOOK AT THESE two jesters and read the inscription 'Wee Three Loggerheads' at the bottom of this seventeenth-century painting, how do you feel as a viewer? Does 'Three Loggerheads' refer to the two fools and their wooden bauble carved with another fool's face? Or, by looking at the painting do *you*, the viewer, become the third 'Loggerhead', immediately included into this group of simpletons? Trick pictures and visual gags like this were popular in early modern England and could be found in a tavern or used as an inn sign. The painting shown here may be an example of the type of 'picture' referred to in Act 2 of *Twelfth Night* when Feste the Jester greets Sir Andrew and Sir Toby, 'How now, my hearts! Did you never see the picture of "we three"?' (2.3.16–17).

The court fool was expected to generate amusement through gluttony, a perceptible lack of intellect and their eccentric physical appearance. Both fools wear a cap with asses' ears fixed to either side. Tom Derry (left), jester to Queen Anne of Denmark, bears a feather on his cap, while Muckle John (right), employed by Charles I, wears a 'coxcomb', a hat shaped like the crest of a cock. Even more striking is Derry's raised right hand, which is depicted with six fingers. Whether he actually had six fingers or if this is a playful addition by the artist is unclear. However, it highlights the association of fools and physical abnormalities frequently seen in paintings. This painting makes us question our perception and understanding of the image, forcing us to wonder whether or not we have been branded as fools.

Figure 5.4 'Wee Three Loggerheads', 1600–25, unknown artist, oil on board, 61cm × 40.6cm, SBT 1994-38.

Writing desk box *no. 38*

DESK BOXES, LIKE THIS EXAMPLE from the early 1600s, also called writing slopes, were portable structures designed to sit on a lap or a table. This particular example is made of English oak and stands 25.5cm high, 41cm long, and 37cm wide, just a little bigger than a full-size laptop computer of today. It has a scrolled book rest, and its front panel and sides are decorated with scratch moulding. Butterfly hinges at the top of the desk secure the slanted lid, and the design allows convenient access to items stored inside the object without disturbing the writing or reading that may have rested on the top. When sitting atop a table and not in use, the desk may have been draped with a Turkish-style table carpet.

Upon visiting Shakespeare's Birthplace, people often ask to see the desk where the famous dramatist wrote and stored his plays. They are surprised to learn that no such object exists, as the kinds of desks with which we are familiar today did not appear until well after William's death, at the end of the seventeenth century. If he did have a preferred place in which to keep his writings it was likely a portable desk box like this. Though this particular example was made for a reasonably affluent owner, one who possessed books and associated furniture, this object is relatively modest and decidedly basic in form and style. It represents the kind of practical object that might have been owned by the professional writers of Elizabethan and Jacobean England.

Figure 5.5 Desk box, 17th century, English, oak, 25.5cm × 41cm × 37cm, SBT 1994-22.

Loveinge Contrieman I am bolde if yo...

... the ... wch ... vppon me my selfe ... proveysse of me ...

... me my kyndnes is now come to London all youre ... f hearte ...

... y part will comyse, yo shall f sende me muche in ...

out of all the dowte I owe in London I thanke god & muche ...

grent my mynde wch wolde now be inteloft I am nowe take ...

the cowrse wch hope & anylure for the disspate of my mynye ...

yo shall not be least readyst noe monnye by me the Lorde &...

wrytinge & now but pswade yo we self he ds I hope & yo...

wyll holde my tyme & rewe ... yo frende & yf we be tryg ...

a me facthe yo shall the pthw... yo self, my tyme be ...

me flepeau to the ende & she romit thy yo care & hope ...

& yor flep I feare f shall now be barke thy myst of som...

the doveny plefe the Lorde be wt yo & wt yo all ...

ff com the well in Cavode lane the 25 octbr 1598 /

yor m all kyndenes

Rychd. Dugend

A letter to Shakespeare   no. 39

T HIS IS THE ONLY KNOWN surviving letter written to Shakespeare. It was discovered in 1793 amongst the many papers of the Stratford-upon-Avon Corporation archives. On the reverse it is addressed to 'To my Loveinge good ffrend & contreymann Mr. Wm Shackespere'. It is dated 'from the Bell in Carter Lane the 25 October 1598' and signed by Richard Quiney.

The Quiney and Shakespeare families were well known to each other in Stratford-upon-Avon. In 1598, Richard Quiney was in London on civic business as town alderman and bailiff. Stratford was experiencing hard times. Bad weather had caused poor harvests and two fires had caused devastation throughout the town; Stratford was also in trouble with the central authorities over the payment of its taxes. In the letter Quiney asks his friend and fellow wealthy townsman for help in raising money to pay the debts he has incurred on behalf of the town: 'Loving countryman, I am bold of you as a friend, craving your help with 30 pounds'. The letter highlights Shakespeare's success and status having established his career and wealth in London; Quiney expects that Shakespeare has sufficient funds to act as moneylender, or sees him as someone able to secure credit in London. The letter also clearly illustrates the two worlds in which Shakespeare had influence, in London but also continuing in Stratford-upon-Avon. The letter is surrounded in mystery; did Shakespeare ever read it, did he ever arrange a loan of £30 for Quiney on behalf of the Corporation of Stratford? As the letter was found in Quiney's own archive, we assume it was never sent to Shakespeare, or perhaps they met in London, rendering the letter unnecessary.

Figure 5.6 Letter from Richard Quiney to William Shakespeare, 25 October 1598, paper, 16.8cm × 13.6cm, SBT ER27/4.

Older Age 6

William Shakespeare's seal-ring? no. 40

THIS REMARKABLE RING HAS A decorated bezel and etched designs on the face. At the top is a true lover's knot, running down to a bowen or heraldic knot, and beneath is a rather clumsy termination which appear to be tassel-like shapes. It is engraved with the initials WS and since its discovery in 1810 in a field adjoining the Holy Trinity churchyard in Stratford-upon-Avon, it has been identified as William Shakespeare's own signet ring.

In the sixteenth and early seventeenth centuries, signet rings were used to imprint the warm wax applied to documents with the sender's symbol – this could be a monogram, a coat of arms or any other recognizable design. Signet derives from the Old French word *signe*, meaning to mark, or a signature. By 1600, signet rings were usually worn on the forefinger or thumb – the latter a fashion revived by Henry VIII. Rings were also worn around the neck on a chain, and many seventeenth-century signets are not ring-forms at all, but simple seals with handles and a hole for a chain. They are usually associated with men of business, to be used in professional situations. John Shakespeare was granted a coat of arms in October 1596 so from this point William was acknowledged to be a gentleman. Given his social status and standing, it is probable that he owned a ring like this.

The provenance of the ring is supported by the fact that Shakespeare did not authenticate his will in 1616 by 'seal' (this word is crossed through) but rather by 'hand' (inserted). If he had lost his ring – folklore suggests he did so in grief after burying his son Hamnet in 1596 – then it is possible that this seal-ring was indeed Shakespeare's.

Figure 6.1 Gold signet ring with 'W S' initials, 17th century, English, gold, 1.6cm × 1.9cm, SBT 1868-3/274.

A die from New Place   no. 41

T HIS TINY DIE IS MADE from bone and measures just 7mm across
– much smaller than a standard modern die. Its numbers have been
carefully and uniformly carved. Dice have been used since before recorded
history, and the oldest known dice were excavated as part of a 5000-year-old
backgammon set in south-eastern Iran.

This die is very special as it was found during archaeological excavations of
the site of Shakespeare's home 'New Place' in 2010. New Place was the
second largest house in Stratford when William Shakespeare bought it in
1597 aged 33, located at the heart of the town next to the Guild Chapel,
the King Edward IV school buildings and the Falcon Inn. When
Shakespeare lived at New Place he was already an established playwright
at the height of his success as a writer, and was a prominent citizen of his
home town. In this, his family home, Shakespeare might well have used a
die like this to play games with his daughters Susanna and Judith or on
evenings when entertaining his friends. This rare find speaks of the
popularity of games using dice during this period such as backgammon,
known as tables, or Quenes where two dice were used and you won by
having the same number appear on both dice. Dice were also used for
gambling, a theme which Shakespeare exploits in many of his plays. Edgar,
in *King Lear* says: 'Wine loved I deeply, dice dearly' (3.4.89–90), while in
Henry IV, Part I, the fun-loving Falstaff remarks: 'Why, there is it: come,
sing me a bawdy song, make me merry. I was as virtuously given as a
gentleman need to be: virtuous enough; swore little; diced not above seven
times a week' (3. 3.13–16).

Figure 6.2 Bone die excavated from the site of
New Place, bone, 0.7cm, SBT 2010–13.

Gentleman's nightcap   *no. 42*

T HIS RICHLY DECORATED GENTLEMAN'S NIGHTCAP dates
from the first quarter of the seventeenth century. It is made from
linen and is embroidered with coloured silks and silver-gilt thread. Patterns
of roses, strawberries and other plants cover the cap, symbolizing beauty
and fertility. These were popular decorations used by the elite in the early
modern period, and donning a nightcap decorated in this manner would
have displayed the wearer's wealth. Nightcaps are rarely seen nowadays,
but in Shakespeare's time more or less everyone would have worn one on a
daily – or rather nightly – basis. The function of these items was not solely
for ensuring warmth in bed, as we might imagine. In fact, nightcaps were
most commonly worn as informal garments around the house in the
evening after the rigours of the day were over. The householder would
change out of his formal or practical day clothes into something more
comfortable, putting on his nightcap in the process. He might even entertain friends while wearing his nightcap: it signified that the time for relax-
ation had come. As such, the nightcap would have been universally
recognizable as a symbol of relaxed domesticity in the Tudor and Stuart
periods. In Shakespeare's *Julius Caesar*, Caska reports the crowd's response
to Caesar's rejection of the crown: 'as he refused it, the rabblement hooted,
and clapped their chopped hands, and threw up their sweaty nightcaps . . .'
(1.2.243–5).

The use of the nightcap as a symbol of plebeian life in this scene would
have conveyed to Shakespeare's audience the momentousness of this occasion, to have drawn these ordinary men from the peace and quiet of their
houses.

Figure 6.3 Gentleman's nightcap, 1601–25, English,
silk, linen and silver, 26.5cm × 23cm, SBT 1994–70.

Posset cup *no. 43*

T HIS HUMBLE LITTLE CUP OR bowl made from earthenware may have been used for drinking posset, a hot drink made from sweetened milk mixed with alcohol, such as ale, wine, or liquor and flavoured with sugar and spices like cinnamon and nutmeg. Throughout the sixteenth and seventeenth centuries posset was thought to possess powerful medicinal and restorative properties, and physicians gave posset to their patients to cure colds and fevers. A printed advertisement of 'Famous and Effectual Medicine to Cure the Plague' from 1665 even lists posset as a remedy for deadly diseases. And when recounting his death, the ghost of Hamlet's father compares the potency of the poison which kills him with the power of posset: 'And with a sudden vigour it does posset / And curd, like eager droppings into milk, / The thin and wholesome blood' (1.5.68–70).

However, its popularity reached beyond its curative abilities. Drinking posset was frequently part of the rituals of entertainment and it was consumed at weddings, feasts and sweet banquets. It was also drunk for pleasure in the evenings with friends and houseguests, similar to our modern day 'nightcap'. In *The Merry Wives of Windsor*, Master Page invites Master Ford to his house to dine on posset: 'Yet be cheerful, knight: thou shalt eat a posset tonight at my house' (5.5.168–9).

Figure 6.4 Posset cup, 16th century, English, earthenware, 15cm × 5cm, SBT 1993–31/399.

Banqueting trencher   *no. 44*

T HIS THIN WOODEN PLATTER IS one of a set of twelve elaborately decorated roundels. Known as 'trenchers', each is painted on one side only with brightly coloured lacework designs, stylized fruits and flowers, and brief, but compelling, proverbial verses. The verse on this trencher reads: 'O death yi / power is great I / must confese I often / wish that it were / lese.' The other side is left bare. Sets of painted trenchers were used in sugar banquets, a special after-dinner or dessert course which took place after the main meal had finished. Sugar banquets were characterized by pageantry and spectacle and were designed to delight the eye rather than satisfy the stomach. During the banquet, a trencher would be placed in front of each guest, the painted side face down, and sweet delicacies such as comfits, marzipan or sugar confectionary would be served on the undecorated side. After the sweets were eaten, guests would turn their trenchers over to reveal the imagery and verse on their trencher and then, it is thought, read them aloud to the table.

It was common for the inscriptions to touch on the moral concerns of daily life and convey warnings against greed, gluttony and profane swearing while virtues such as charity, sobriety and patience were encouraged. Not surprisingly, verses often incorporated biblical passages. In addition to being beautifully decorated objects designed for social entertainment at what were spectacular and often whimsical banquets, trenchers also articulated weightier moral concerns, as well as practical wisdom, and acted as prompts for more serious contemplation.

Figure 6.5 One of a set of twelve banqueting trenchers, 1597, English, sycamore, pasteboard, vellum and paper, 13cm × 0.3cm, SBT 1992–4.

Pocket dial no. 45

Successful, professional people in Shakespeare's England needed to be able to tell the time on the move. This pocket or ring dial dates to around 1600 and is made from brass. It is engraved on the inside with the hours of the day and on the outside with the initials of the months. A pierced, sliding ring runs around the middle, and in order to tell the time the hole in this sliding band would be lined up with the month on the outside of the dial. When held up to the light, the sun would shine through this hole and onto the correct hour engraved on the inside, thus giving a (fairly) accurate indication of the time. Although the value of clocks and pocket dials varied greatly, they were nonetheless regarded as luxury items and something of a status symbol. As a result, dials such as this one might be worn hung around the neck and displayed on the outside of clothing, in order to show off the item to the greatest number of people. However, they were also small enough to be carried around in one's pocket, as the name suggests, and as Jaques indicates in *As You Like It*:

> A fool, a fool! I met a fool i' th' forest,
> A motley fool . . .
> And then he drew a dial from his poke [pocket],
> And looking on it with lack-lustre eye
> Says, very wisely, 'It is ten o'clock.'
> (2.7.12–22)

Jaques' comment here indicates both Shakespeare's familiarity with the item and his understanding of its social significance: the very idea of a 'fool' owning a pocket dial and worrying about the time would have been amusing to his audience.

Figure 6.6 Pocket dial, 17th century, English, copper alloy, 5.75cm (diam.), SBT 1910–14.

Death 7

Memento mori seal impression   *no. 46*

Making a 'good' death in Elizabethan and Jacobean England was very important, because it signalled the destination of your soul. People were encouraged to live an honest life, to repent their sins, and to pray and meditate daily. One of the prompts used to encourage this reflection on death was the *memento mori*. 'Memento mori' is Latin for 'remember you must die', and this phrase could be inscribed on any number of objects. It often appeared alongside a skull (or 'death's head'), as in the wax seal impression featured here. This impression also includes the initials 'N.R.', which may have belonged to the seal's owner, who we can imagine being reminded of his own mortality every time he sealed a letter. Falstaff refers to the *memento mori* tradition in *Henry IV, Part I*, in which he likens Bardolph's red face to the fires of hell:

BARDOLPH: Why, Sir John, my face does you no harm.
FALSTAFF: No, I'll be sworn, I make as good use of it as many a man doth of a death's head, or a *memento mori*. I never see thy face but I think upon hell-fire . . .

(3.3.28–31)

Today we would find this kind of preoccupation with death decidedly morbid; however for the people of Shakespeare's England, when death might snatch you away at any point, it was always prudent to be prepared for judgement and there could be a comfort in looking forward to eternal life.

Figure 7.1 Seal bearing the impression of death's head and the legend 'N.R. Momento Mori', 17th century, wax, 2.7cm × 2.2cm, SBT 1872–4.

MORS VLTIMA LINEA
RERVM EST

Painting of 'Death and the Maiden'

no. 47

T HIS PAINTING IN OIL ON panel is by an unknown English artist and dates to around 1570. A young woman strums a lute, a symbol of harmony, learning and pleasure. She wears an embroidered bodice, with gown and fine damasked under-skirt, fashionable 'slashed' sleeves, and a small head-dress beneath a spectacular feathered hat. In stark contrast with her youthful opulence is an elderly man who holds a convex mirror in his left hand. In his right hand he swings a skull over the woman's shoulder: her reflected image, should she choose to look at it, sits alongside an image of death. In the top right-hand corner of the picture, a line in Latin from Horace's *Epistles* (1, 16, 79) translates loosely as 'Death is everything's final limit'.

This type of painting is known as a *vanitas* – from Ecclesiastes 1: 2, 'vanity of vanities; all is vanity'. It is part of the *memento mori* visual tradition which reminded viewers that despite wealth, power, beauty or indeed poverty, death awaits all and is the great leveller. In the Catholic tradition, these served as warnings against greed and excessive indulgent pleasure. But the treatment of the subject here is quite different.

The woman does not engage the reflection held before her, but stares soberly and intently at the viewer. She is not lewdly dressed – as women generally are in earlier treatments of this theme. She encourages the viewer to consider death as the ultimate release, not from worldliness and vanity particularly, but from the limit put on true pleasure by human frailty. This sentiment, glimpsed throughout Shakespeare's works, is distilled here in an elegant and complex work that could prompt contemplation.

Figure 7.2 'Death and the Maiden', c.1570, unknown artist, English, oil on board, 65cm × 49cm, SBT 1993–30.

Medicine chest   no. 48

T HIS CHEST IS DECORATED WITH an inlay of holly and black bog oak, and was probably made by immigrant German artisans working in London in the 1580s. The interior of the lid is pasted with printed wallpaper with grotesque motifs and strapwork designs and dates to the same decade. The interior is compact and has numerous small partitions, drawers operated by silk pulls, and even a secret compartment. It is an exceptionally fine piece of craftsmanship and is consistent with other surviving examples of medicine chests from the early modern period.

Shakespeare died, according to folklore, after a night of heavy drinking in nearby Bidford-on-Avon. We know that he made a will in Stratford, leaving his worldly possessions to his family and friends. John Hall, Shakespeare's son-in-law and a Stratford physician, perhaps treated Shakespeare at New Place using the typical tools of the trade – urine flasks and the ancient technique of uroscopy. This medicine chest, by virtue of its size, could not accommodate these flasks and therefore is almost certainly not a physicians' chest. It is instead a receptacle for 'kitchen physic', garden herbs and other everyday medical materials that were used by women to remedy the day-to-day ills of their households in the late sixteenth century.

It is probable that throughout Shakespeare's life and in his final illness, he was treated by his wife and daughters, whose knowledge of kitchen physic and a culture of 'receipts' – medicinal cures passed on by word of mouth and eventually transcribed by gentlewomen in receipt books – helped to alleviate his suffering.

Figure 7.3 Medicine chest, 1550–1625, English, oak and holly, 39.5cm × 20cm × 26cm, SBT 2001–5.

616

1	A Infant of garr ...
2	Ales vxor garr ...
3	Katheren vxor ... Iremonll
5	Ioan vxor mill ... affer
9	Ioyr fillia ... Arthur
9	margret fillia Fraunces Swayn
15	margret wheelas ... wid

Aprill
3	Thomas dinson
5	margret fillia Iohn Iames
9	ton thomas of ... huseman
15	mill dauid Kent
16	A Infant of tho madiward
17	will hartt haller ✗
21	Elizabeth fillia mill framer
23	An Corke widow
24	Richard pynder
25	will Chatspare Kent ✗

maij
9	margret fillia robert ... plumer
11	ton Lwines of mill ... mouse
23	Thomas bramley de royton
25	Thomas bradshed ... winlaton

1	Alie bearude widow
4	An Kert widow
14	Elizabeth Cuninge
18	Alie fillia Roger ... midllenge
21	A Infant of Robert ward
26	Peter midlenes
26	Thomas fillius henry pratt
30	Thomas fillius tho: lemilon

Iuly
6	willm Coranll butcher
22	willm Iones
22	thomas fillius tho: Iarkman
26	hinmghuey ... Allin de old stratton
28	Iohn fillius Iohn Gwen ...
28	Steben fillius Edward perse ...
28	Katheren fillia Iohn Coatts
	Alie vxor Edmund perse de ...

Parish register

T HIS IS THE EARLIEST SURVIVING parish register of Holy Trinity
Church, Stratford-upon-Avon. Though partially rebound on several
occasions during its lifetime, it retains parts of the original binding
including its brown leather cover. It has brass corner-pieces decorated with
the Tudor Rose, and remnants of brass clasps. The volume bears the date
1600 when a new official regulation required that the original paper
register, which had been in use since the 1530s, be copied into a new sturdy
volume made of parchment. All entries prior to 1600, dating back to 1558,
including four references to Shakespeare and his children, were copied
into the register in the same hand. The parish register has long been of
interest to Shakespeare scholars and enthusiasts alike and it was for a time
on permanent display in Holy Trinity Church.

Here we can see the entry recording the burial of 'Will Shakspere gent.' on
25 April 1616; he was 52. He is given the title of gentleman, indicating the
status he had achieved; a title which was only used by a small number of
his fellow townsmen. Tradition has it that he had died two days earlier, but
the actual date and cause of his death is not known. Many years later in
1661, the vicar of Stratford-upon-Avon noted in his diary: 'Shakespeare,
Drayton, and Ben Jonson had a merry meeting, and it seems drank too
hard; for Shakespeare died of a fever there contracted.' But some scholars
believe that he had been sick for over a month. On 25 March 1616,
Shakespeare signed his last will and testament, as was then customary by
those close to death.

Figure 7.4 Parish register, Holy Trinity Church, Stratford-
upon-Avon. Register of Baptisms, showing William Shakespeare's
burial record, 1558–1653, 43cm × 18cm, SBT DR243/1.

Shakespeare's bust   *no. 50*

OUR FINAL OBJECT BRINGS us face to face with William Shakespeare. It is a plaster cast, made in 1814, of the bust from his monument in Holy Trinity church in Stratford. The monument was erected sometime after Shakespeare's death and before the publication of the First Folio in 1623, where one of the prefatory poems mentions 'thy Stratford monument'. The effigy bust, like the other famous posthumous image of the author contained in the First Folio, is accepted as an accurate record of his physical appearance as he would have looked in later life.

Funeral monuments were set up in huge numbers in Elizabethan and Jacobean England; memorials were central to an expanding culture of commemoration. Only people of some status were permitted memorials in church and Shakespeare's monument on the north wall of the chancel reflects his privileged position as a leading citizen of his town. The form of the sculpted stone monument is of a type favoured for scholars or divines and the inscription in Latin and English praises his genius and artistry as a writer. A few abbreviated words in Latin states he died on 23 April 1616.

The monument has been subject to various alterations, with major interventions in 1748, 1793 (when the effigy was overpainted in white) and 1861, but it is not thought the face has been substantially altered. As with the houses and collections cared for by the Shakespeare Birthplace Trust, Shakespeare's monument is a focus of global interest, which embeds and enshrines his memory within his home town. This copy made in 1814 is special in being cast directly from the monument and (unlike the original version located high up on the wall) it allows us to directly meet his gaze.

Figure 7.5 Cast of William Shakespeare's bust from his monument in Holy Trinity Church, 1814, George Bullock, plaster, 82cm × 67cm × 82cm, SBT 1868–3/280.

Key dates in the life of William Shakespeare

1558 Elizabeth I ascends to the throne – the Elizabethan age begins.

1559 The Elizabethan Religious Settlement establishes the Protestant faith in England.

26 April 1564 William Shakespeare, son of John and Mary, is baptised at Holy Trinity Church in Stratford-upon-Avon.

c.1569–71 Shakespeare goes to the grammar school in Stratford.

28 November 1582 Marriage of William Shakespeare, aged 18, to Anne Hathaway.

26 May 1583 Baptism of Susanna Shakespeare.

2 February 1585 Baptism of twins, son Hamnet and daughter Judith.

1590 Around this time, Shakespeare relocates to London and starts to write for the stage.

January 1593 Plague closes playhouses.

April 1593 Publication of Shakespeare's poem 'Venus and Adonis'.

11 August 1596 Burial of son Hamnet, aged 11.

October 1596 The College of Heralds grant a coat of arms to John Shakespeare.

May 1597 Shakespeare buys New Place in Stratford.

1599 The Globe Theatre is built in Southwark by Shakespeare's acting company, the Lord Chamberlain's Men.

8 September 1601 Burial of Shakespeare's father, John.

24 March 1603 Queen Elizabeth I dies; King James I ascends the throne.

5 June 1607 Shakespeare's daughter Susanna marries John Hall in Holy Trinity Church.

21 February 1608 Baptism of Shakespeare's granddaughter Elizabeth Hall.

9 September 1608 Burial of Shakespeare's mother, Mary Arden.

1609 Publication of Shakespeare's sonnets.

25 March 1616 Shakespeare writes his will.

23 April 1616 Shakespeare dies, aged 52.

25 April 1616 Burial in Holy Trinity Church. Within the next few years a funeral monument is set up marking his burial in the chancel.

1623 Publication of First Folio of Shakespeare's collected plays.

Credits and references

Stephanie Appleton (objects 7, 14, 18, 20, 21, 22, 25, 31, 36, 42, 45, 46); Delia Garratt (objects 9, 10, 15, 34, 35, 39, 41, 49); Tara Hamling (general editor and objects 1, 23, 28, 50); Peter Hewitt (objects 2, 3, 4, 5, 6, 8, 19, 24, 29, 40, 47, 48); Victoria Jackson (objects 16, 17, 30, 33, 37, 43, 44); Elizabeth Sharrett (objects 11, 12, 13, 26, 27, 32, 38). All images © The Shakespeare Birthplace Trust.

References

In the overarching themes and arrangement of objects within the present volume, we have responded to recent academic work on material culture, the lifecycle and rites of passage. It is impossible to reference the full range of work in this area but the sources listed below have informed directly our information and interpretation: Chinnery, Victor (1988), *Oak Furniture: The British Tradition* (Antique Collectors Club); Franits, Wayne, 'The Family Saying Grace: A Theme in Dutch Art of the Seventeenth Century', *Simiolus* vol. 16. no. 1 (1986): 36–49. Hewitt, Peter (2015) 'The material culture of Shakespeare's England: a study of the early modern objects in the museum collection of the Shakespeare Birthplace Trust', Ph.D. thesis, University of Birmingham; Hamling, Tara and Richardson, Catherine, eds (2010) *Everyday Objects: Medieval and Early Modern Material Culture and its Meanings* (Ashgate); Hamling, Tara (2010) *Decorating the Godly Household: Religious Art in Protestant Britain* (Yale University Press); Harrison, William (1587) *The Description of England*, ed. Georges Edelen (Dover Publications, 1994); Llewellyn, Nigel (1991), *The Art of Death: Visual Culture in the English Death Ritual, c.1500–1800* (Reaktion books); Macgregor, Neil (2014) *Shakespeare's Restless World: An Unexpected History in Twenty Objects* (Penguin); Mulryne, J.R. (2012), *The Guild and Guild Buildings of Shakespeare's Stratford* (Ashgate); O'Hara (2002), *Courtship and Constraint: Rethinking the Making of Marriage in Tudor England* (Manchester University Press, 2002); Pitcairn, Robert ed. (1833) *Ancient Criminal Trials in Scotland* (Bannatyne Club); Richardson, Catherine (2011), *Shakespeare and Material Culture* (Oxford University Press); Strong, Roy (1987) *Gloriana: The Portraits of Queen Elizabeth I* (Thames and Hudson); Thompson, Ann, ed. (2011), *Arden Shakespeare Complete Works* (Bloomsbury).

Websites

Bate, Jonathan and the Shakespeare Birthplace Trust, 'Shakespeare and his World', online course: https://www.futurelearn.com/courses/shakespeare-and-his-world; various authors, 'Shakespeare's World in 100 Objects', Finding Shakespeare online blog: http://findingshakespeare.co.uk/category/shakespeares-100; 'Windows on Warwickshire' website, http://www.windowsonwarwickshire.org.uk/